8/06

CORI DERKSEN AND MYRA HARDER

The
Blessed Home
Quilt

DISCARD

And Other Learn-as-You-Sew Projects

Martingale®
& COMPANY

The Blessed Home Quilt:
And Other Learn-as-You-Sew Projects
© 2006 by Cori Derksen and
Myra Harder

That Patchwork Place® is an imprint
of Martingale & Company®.

Martingale & Company
20205 144th Avenue NE
Woodinville, WA 98072-8478 USA
www.martingale-pub.com

Printed in China
11 10 09 08 07 06   8 7 6 5 4 3 2 1

**Library of Congress Cataloging-
Publication Data**
Derkson, Cori.
   The blessed home quilt : and
other learn-as-you-sew projects /
Cori Derkson and Myra Harder.
      p. cm.
   ISBN 1-56477-666-2
 1. Patchwork—Patterns.
 2. Quilting. 3. Samplers.
 4. Patchwork quilts. I. Harder, M
 II. Title.
   TT835.D46298 2006
   746.46'041—dc22
                                   200503

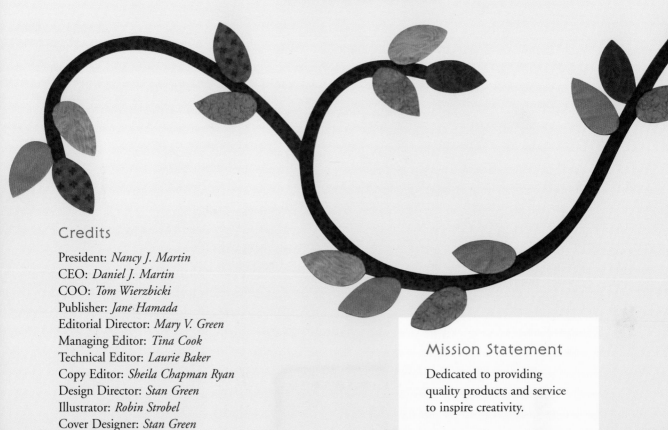

Credits

President: *Nancy J. Martin*
CEO: *Daniel J. Martin*
COO: *Tom Wierzbicki*
Publisher: *Jane Hamada*
Editorial Director: *Mary V. Green*
Managing Editor: *Tina Cook*
Technical Editor: *Laurie Baker*
Copy Editor: *Sheila Chapman Ryan*
Design Director: *Stan Green*
Illustrator: *Robin Strobel*
Cover Designer: *Stan Green*
Text Designer: *Trina Craig*
Photographer: *Brent Kane*

Mission Statement

Dedicated to providing
quality products and service
to inspire creativity.

Acknowledgments

Our sincere thanks and appreciation go to:

- RJR Fabrics, for providing a great selection of fabrics for the creation of an array of projects

- Jacqueline Pohl, from the Vintage Quiltery in Gladstone, Manitoba, for her beautiful machine quilting and bringing another dimension to our "Blessed Home Sampler Quilt"

- Karen Greaves, from Ignace, Ontario, for machine quilting "Prairie Lap Quilt"—her time and creativity made a simple quilt look elegant

- Betty Klassen, for her support and willingness to machine quilt on short notice

Contents

Introduction

THE IDEA FOR a sampler quilt specifically designed for learning basic quiltmaking techniques began several years ago when we heard a customer in a quilt store make an interesting comment. She simply said, "Just because I'm a beginning quilter doesn't mean that I'm not willing to put time into a big project. I just need it at my skill level." It occurred to us that many projects for beginners are very simple, unimaginative, and designed to be done quickly. We've even known some quilters who have been too embarrassed to show others their early projects because the designs wouldn't fit into their homes, but they made them because they were at their skill level.

With those thoughts in mind, we started designing a project that we thought quilters would be proud of when they were finished with it, and then we broke the project down into basic lessons. This book was the result of those efforts. We believe that even if you've never quilted before, you can work your way through each lesson, and when you're finished, you'll have a complete understanding of all of the basics of quiltmaking. After each lesson, we've provided a project so that you can practice your new skills. The lessons are followed by the "Blessed Home Sampler Quilt" instructions, in which all of the new techniques are used. In the end, you'll have made a number of great projects in all different sizes, as well as an attractive sampler quilt to display!

Even though this book is geared toward beginners, it doesn't mean advanced quilters won't find something of interest in the projects. You can still enjoy the fun of working toward the "Blessed Home Sampler Quilt" no matter what your skill level. In fact, you might want to consider using this book as a tool for teaching someone who admires your work. There's something here for everyone!

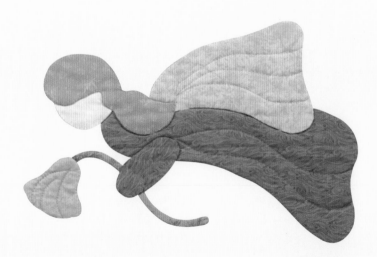

THE SUPPLIES LISTED here are the essential items you will need for making the quilts in this book.

Fabric. Cotton is the number one choice! We find working with cotton fabric to be the least frustrating and the most rewarding. Cotton quilts will last for many generations, so many people will be able to enjoy your work for years to come.

We encourage you to change the colorways of the projects to suit your own taste, style, or decor. Changing colors may transform a piece that you were not drawn to at first into a quilt that you love and that truly becomes your own masterpiece. "Step out of the box" and use colors that you normally don't choose. Be creative. Be daring. Just don't get caught in a rut!

One of the best features of the "Blessed Home Sampler Quilt" is the number of fabrics it uses. Your fabric selection will make your quilt interesting and also your personal creation. We used 26 fabrics in this quilt, but don't feel overwhelmed. When you break the quilt down and study what you need, it won't be hard to make good choices.

Many quilters ask whether they need to prewash their fabrics. This is unnecessary if you are using quality fabrics. In the past, when most cotton fabrics were lower quality, prewashing was necessary because the fabric could shrink considerably. This is still a reason to be careful of loosely woven cottons from an unknown source. Because minor shrinkage can occur in any cotton fabric, it is important not to mix cottons with polyester-and-cotton blends, which may not have any shrinkage at all. Mixing fabrics of various blends can cause puckers.

Thread. Use a good-quality, 50-weight, three-ply cotton or polyester all-purpose thread for piecing. Avoid the bins of "bargain" thread that you often see at discount stores. The majority of these threads are made from inferior fibers that shred, break, and cause havoc for your machine and frustration for you.

Paper-piecing paper. The project that accompanies the lesson on paper piecing and some of the elements of the "Blessed Home Sampler Quilt" are paper pieced. The patterns for paper piecing need to be transferred to a paper that is lightweight and tears away from the fabric seams easily. During the past few years, several papers have been designed specifically for this purpose. You can find them in many quilting stores. In a pinch, you can use typing or printer paper. You will need to be careful with it when you tear away the paper because it is a little heavier and it can pull and loosen your seams.

Freezer paper. We use an appliqué method in which the patterns are made from freezer paper. Our favorite freezer paper for appliqué can be found on grocery-store shelves across America. You may even have some in your cupboard. It is a white paper that comes on a roll like aluminum foil. One side of the paper is plain and the other side has a smooth, waxy coating. This paper works well because you can see through it to trace the pattern, unlike the brown wax paper that is common in our native Canada. When it is heated with an iron, the waxy coating gently sticks to the fabric.

Appliqué and quilting needles. Your local quilt shop will have a variety of hand-sewing needles. The major difference in needles is the size of the eye and the length of the shaft. When teaching students, we always suggest beginning with a size 10 needle for both appliqué and quilting. We find this is the easiest for students to handle. As time goes on and your stitches get smaller, try using a smaller needle.

Scissors. You will need a pair of good-quality scissors for cutting fabric and another less expensive pair for cutting paper. To protect your investment and to keep your scissors sharp, do not use your fabric scissors for cutting paper. Be sure everyone in the house knows that your fabric scissors are for fabric only!

Rotary cutter, mat, and ruler. The rotary cutter was one of the best inventions to ever happen to the quilting industry. Shaped like a pizza cutter, this rolling razor blade saves countless hours that would have once been spent cutting shapes with scissors. The cutters are available in four sizes: 18 mm, 28 mm, 45 mm, and 60 mm. We are most comfortable using the 45 mm size. No matter which company makes the cutter, you will find that spare blades are made to accommodate all the different types. You will also find some cutters with curved handles, designed to be more ergonomic for your hand. Try out as many as you can and find out what fits you best.

When you are using a rotary cutter, you should always cut on a rotary-cutting mat and guide the cutter against a clear rotary ruler. Again, you have many options. By working in a quilting store, we have come to realize that almost everything can be done with one good mat and ruler.

The most important feature in a mat is to make sure that it is at least 24" wide. The reason for this is that fabric off the bolt is between 40" and 44" wide. In order to cut your fabric as one piece, you need a mat that is wider than the fabric when it is folded in half. A 24" x 24" or 24" x 36" mat will be large enough to handle the folded width of the fabric. After you have been quilting for awhile and you are more familiar with your sewing needs, you may want to buy a smaller mat that you can keep beside your machine for quick cutting tasks.

Like the mat, we suggest buying a ruler that is 24" long so that you can cut across the folded width of the fabric. Our favorite is a 6" x 24" ruler. This one basic ruler will meet almost all of your needs. It was the one and only ruler that we used for many years. Over time, we have acquired a few smaller rulers, but we often use these for checking measurements rather than cutting. It can also be handy to have a 1" x 6" ruler beside your machine to check the seam allowances and finished block sizes.

THE FIRST STEP in quilting is learning how to cut out the pieces that will be used to construct your quilt. Most of the pieces for the projects in this book are cut out using rotary-cutting methods that don't use any patterns. A few irregularly shaped pieces in the "Blessed Home Sampler Quilt" will need to be cut out using the measurements given in a diagram. The cutting instructions for those pieces will be given with the project. The cutting methods for curved pieces and appliqué motifs will be given in the chapters that pertain to those techniques.

Before you begin cutting, it is helpful to understand the grain-line terms that are used throughout the instructions. Grain line refers to the direction of the fabric yarns. When you look at a piece of fabric, there are three directions to consider—crosswise, lengthwise, and bias.

Crosswise grain. This refers to the yarns that run from selvage to selvage, or from finished edge to finished edge. The crosswise grain has some amount of give and can stretch a little. If you ever need to make a block a bit bigger, just pull gently on the crosswise grain as you're pressing. When you prewash your fabric, you'll find that the fabric shrinks very little along the crosswise grain and will remain about the same width as when you started.

Lengthwise grain. The yarns that run parallel to the selvage are more stable than the crosswise yarns—they stretch very little. Some quilters prefer to cut the outer borders along the lengthwise grain so that the edges won't stretch or "wave." You'll notice the lengthwise grain shrinks the most when washed.

Bias. Bias intersects the crosswise and lengthwise grains. This is the direction that will stretch the most. The bias can be hard to work with when piecing blocks; however, it is wonderful for appliqué work.

When you cut a square in half to make half-square triangles, the long sides of the triangles will always be on the bias, and you may notice when you sew one to another triangle that the long side can be very stretchy and pull out of shape easily. For this reason, you want to handle bias edges very carefully. However, when making stems, vines, or anything you want to curve, the bias will help you out because it does stretch. The bias of a fabric will be unaffected by prewashing.

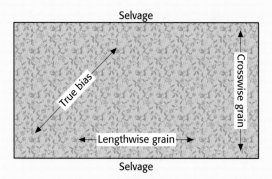

HELPFUL HINT

How do you efficiently cut out your shapes? Always start by cutting the largest pieces first. The cutting instructions for the projects in this book will reflect this.

Straightening the Fabric

Before you begin cutting the pieces, you will need to straighten the raw edges of the fabric. Begin by folding the fabric in half along the lengthwise grain, aligning the selvages. Lay the folded fabric on the cutting mat with the fold closest to you.

Place a 6" x 24" ruler on the right-hand end of the fabric. Align a horizontal line of the ruler with the folded edge of the fabric. Position the ruler only as far in from the raw edges as needed to cut through both layers of fabric. Cut along the edge of the ruler, through both layers of fabric. Discard the cut piece. (Reverse the layout if you are left-handed.) You are now ready to cut strips, squares, rectangles, and triangles.

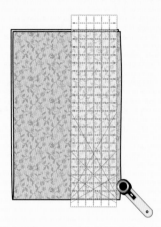

Cutting Strips

Rotate the fabric or mat so that the straightened edge is to your left and the bulk of the fabric is to your right. Cut strips the width given in the pattern instructions, measuring from the straightened edge. For example, if you need a 2½"-wide strip, place the 2½" vertical line of the ruler on the straightened edge of the fabric. Cut along the right side of the ruler. All strips should be cut across the width of the fabric.

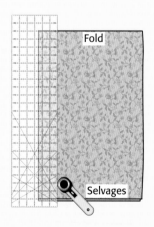

Cutting Squares and Rectangles

Once you have the strips cut, you can crosscut them into squares and rectangles. Lay a folded strip on the cutting mat with the selvage ends to the right. Cut off and straighten the selvage ends of the folded strip by aligning a horizontal line of the ruler with the long edge of the folded strip, like you did for the whole fabric piece. Then with the strip still folded, reposition the straightened edge to your left and measure the required distance from the end of the strip to cut your pieces.

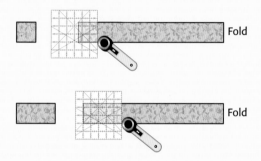

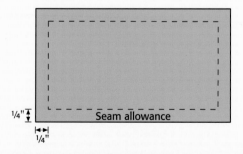

The project cutting instructions will indicate the size to cut your strips, squares, or rectangles. For calculation purposes, we have assumed that you will have 40" of usable fabric width after prewashing and trimming the selvages.

The cut size of a square or rectangle is based on this simple equation:

$$\text{Finished size} + \tfrac{1}{2}" = \text{cut size}$$

For example, if you need a 3" finished square, you should cut a 3½" x 3½" square. This gives you a 3" square with a ¼" seam allowance on all four sides.

If you need a rectangle with a finished size of 3" x 5", you would cut a 3½" x 5½" rectangle. This gives you a rectangle that is 3" x 5" with a ¼" seam allowance on all four sides.

Cutting Triangles from a Square

There are two types of triangles that can be cut from a square: half-square triangles and quarter-square triangles.

Half-square triangles. A half-square triangle is created when you cut a square in half diagonally from one corner to the opposite corner. The cut will yield two triangles. The cut edge, which is the longest side of each triangle, is on the bias.

The equation for determining the size to cut the squares is:

Finished triangle size (uncut edge) + ⅞" = cut size

For example, if you need a triangle that measures 3" across its two short sides, cut a 3⅞" x 3⅞" square and cut it once diagonally to yield two triangles.

Quarter-square triangles. By cutting diagonally across a square in both directions, you'll get four triangles. The two cut edges of each triangle are on the bias.

The formula for determining the size to cut the square is:

Finished triangle size (uncut edge) + 1¼" = cut size

For example, if you need a triangle that measures 3" along its long side, cut a 4¼" x 4¼" square and cut it twice diagonally to yield four triangles.

Lesson One
Technique: *Strip Piecing*

STRIP PIECING IS one of the best quilting techniques to learn first. It is easy to make blocks by sewing strips together, cutting them into smaller segments, and sewing the segments together.

The technique is most easily demonstrated by making the basic Nine Patch block. Many nonquilters may think that this block is made by sewing nine separate squares together to form a finished block. However, by using the strip-piecing method, the block is reduced to a few simple steps.

The first thing you must do to prepare to make a Nine Patch block is to determine the strip width. To do this, determine the *vertical* size of the finished block and divide by three. Add ½" to this measurement, and this will be the width to cut the strips. Cut three strips from a dark fabric and three strips from a light fabric; then follow the steps below to assemble the block.

1. Sew a dark strip to each long edge of a light strip as shown. This is called a strip set. Press the seams toward the dark strips. You will now cut vertically across the strip set to create segments. This is often referred to as crosscutting. To determine the width to cut the segments, measure the horizontal size of the finished block, divide by three, and add ½". (If the finished block is square, this number will be the same as the cut width of the strips before they were sewn together.) You will need two segments for each Nine Patch block.

2. Sew a light strip to each long edge of the remaining dark strip. Press the seams toward the dark strip. Using the width determined in step 1, crosscut one segment for each Nine Patch block.

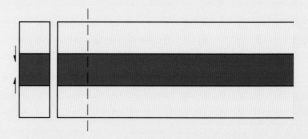

3. To form the finished block, sew a segment from step 1 to each side of a segment from step 2 as shown. You can press the seams either away from the center segment or toward it.

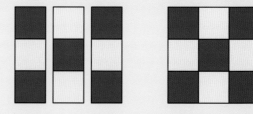

Review Project
Prairie Lap Quilt

Pieced and quilted by Karen Greaves

This easy-to-make lap quilt is the perfect accent piece for throwing over a chair to add a decorator element to your family room. Consider adding detailed quilting to give the simple piecing an elegant look.

Finished quilt size: 57" x 72"
Finished block sizes: 7½" x 15"; 7½" x 7½"

Materials

Yardage is based on 42"-wide fabric, and we've assumed you'll have 40" of usable width after prewashing and trimming selvages. The yardage requirements allow a 10% cushion for shrinkage and for cutting errors.

1¼ yards of multicolored print for outer border
1 yard of light tan fabric for blocks and inner border
⅞ yard of dark green fabric for blocks
¾ yard of dark red fabric for blocks
⅔ yard of light peach fabric for blocks
½ yard of medium peach fabric for blocks
½ yard of light green fabric for blocks
⅝ yard of fabric for binding
3⅔ yards of fabric for backing
61" x 76" piece of batting

Cutting

All measurements include ¼"-wide seam allowances.

From the light tan, cut:
6 strips, 3" x width of fabric
2 strips, 2¾" x width of fabric; crosscut the strips into 24 squares, 2¾" x 2¾". Cut each square once diagonally to yield 48 triangles.
6 strips, 1½" x width of fabric

From the light peach, cut:
7 strips, 3" x width of fabric

From the light green, cut:
5 strips, 3" x width of fabric

From the dark red, cut:
2 strips, 8¾" x width of fabric; crosscut the strips into 6 squares, 8¾" x 8¾". Cut each square twice diagonally to yield 24 triangles.
1 strip, 3⅛" x width of fabric; crosscut the strip into 12 squares, 3⅛" x 3⅛"

From the dark green, cut:
2 strips, 8¾" x width of fabric; crosscut the strips into 6 squares, 8¾" x 8¾". Cut each square twice diagonally to yield 24 large triangles.
3 strips, 3½" x width of fabric; crosscut the strips into 24 squares, 3½" x 3½". Cut each square once diagonally to yield 48 small triangles.

From the medium peach, cut:
3 strips, 4¾" x width of fabric; crosscut the strips into 24 squares, 4¾" x 4¾". Cut each square once diagonally to yield 48 triangles.

From the multicolored print, cut:
7 strips, 5½" x width of fabric

From the binding fabric, cut:
7 strips, 2½" x width of fabric

Making the Blocks

1. To make the Strata blocks, sew a 3"-wide light tan strip to each long side of a light peach strip to make a strip set. Make three. Press the seams toward the peach strips. Crosscut the strip sets into 15½"-wide segments to make six Strata blocks.

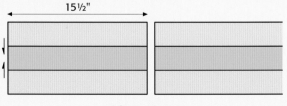

Make 3 strip sets.
Cut 6 segments.

2. To make the Nine Patch blocks, sew a light green strip to each long side of a light peach strip to make a strip set. Make two. Press the seams toward the light green strips. Crosscut the strip sets into 24 segments, 3" wide.

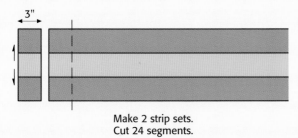

Make 2 strip sets.
Cut 24 segments.

3. Sew a light peach strip to each long side of a light green strip to make a strip set. Press the seams toward the light green strip. Crosscut the strip set into 12 segments, 3" wide.

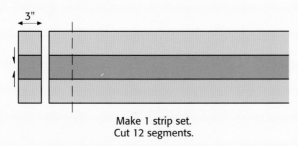

Make 1 strip set.
Cut 12 segments.

4. Join a unit from step 2 to each side of a unit from step 3 as shown to make a Nine Patch block. Press the seams away from the center segments. Make 12.

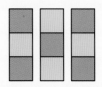

Nine Patch block.
Make 12.

5. To make the Square-in-a-Square blocks, fold the dark red squares in half lengthwise and crosswise to find the center of each side. Fold the light tan triangles, the small dark green triangles, and the medium peach triangles in half along the long edges to find the centers.

6. Sew light tan triangles to opposite sides of each dark red square, matching the centers. Press the seams toward the triangles. Sew light tan triangles to the remaining sides of each square, again matching the centers and pressing the seams toward the triangles.

7. Repeat step 6 with the dark green triangles and then the medium peach triangles to complete the Square-in-a-Square blocks. Make 12.

 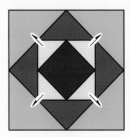

Square-in-a-Square block.
Make 12.

8. To make the Hourglass blocks, sew each large dark green triangle to a dark red triangle along the short edges. Sew two units together as shown. Make 12.

Hourglass block.
Make 12.

Assembling the Quilt Top

1. Arrange the blocks into seven horizontal rows of six blocks each as shown. Make sure you rotate every other Hourglass block 90° as shown. Sew the blocks together into rows, and then sew the rows together.

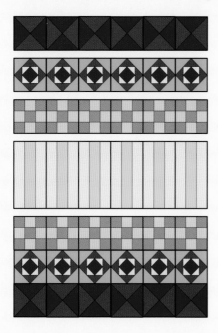

2. Refer to "Adding Borders" on page 60 to sew the light tan 1½"-wide strips together end to end to make one long strip. From the pieced strip, cut two strips, 1½" x 60½", for the side inner borders and two strips, 1½" x 47½", for the top and bottom inner borders. Sew the side inner borders to the quilt top first; then sew the top and bottom inner borders to the quilt top as shown above right.

3. Sew the multicolored print strips together end to end to make one long strip. From the pieced strip, cut two strips, 5½" x 62½", for the side outer borders and two strips, 5½" x 57½", for the top and bottom outer borders. Sew the side outer borders to the quilt top first; then sew the top and bottom outer borders to the quilt top as shown above right.

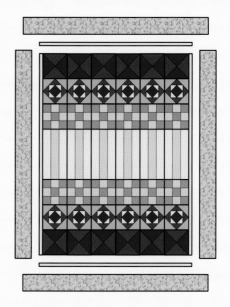

Finishing the Quilt

For detailed instructions on finishing techniques, refer to "Finishing Techniques" on page 60.

1. Cut and piece the backing fabric so that it is 4" to 6" larger than the quilt top. Layer the quilt top with batting and backing. Baste the layers together.

2. Hand or machine quilt as desired.

3. Prepare and sew the binding to the quilt.

4. Block the quilt to square it up.

QUILTING SUGGESTIONS

Simple piecing does not mean you have to use a simple quilting design. By using an elegant wreath motif and enhancing it with stippling, our machine quilter, Karen Greaves, added texture and character to this future heirloom.

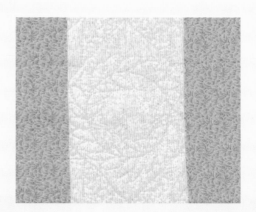

Lesson Two
Technique: *Curved Piecing*

MANY PEOPLE ENJOY the look curved pieces give to quilts, but they are too intimidated to try sewing the pieces. Sewing curves is really just as easy as sewing a straight line; it just takes a little more attention and a few more moments of preparation, but the results are worth it.

Most curved pieces are cut with the aid of a template. We recommend using template plastic to make your templates. Template plastic is easy to see through for tracing the pattern, is easy to cut, and will retain its shape over time. To make a template, simply trace the pattern for the shape onto template plastic using a fine-line permanent marker. Cut out the template on the outer line. The seam allowance has already been added to the patterns in this book.

The most important rules in curved piecing are to mark the centers of the pieces and to use pins! Always mark the centers of the concave and convex pieces. To find the center, fold the piece in half along the curved edge. Crease the edge at the center or mark it with a pin or fabric marker. Lay the pieces on top of each other, right sides together, and then pin the pieces together at the centers and ends. Slowly sew from one end to the other using a ¼" seam allowance; gently ease the fabrics together. The curved edges are cut on the bias, which allows you to ease the two different curves to meet.

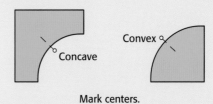

Mark centers.

Don't be intimidated by curves! Understand how easy they can be and you'll begin to look at curved blocks in a new light.

HELPFUL HINT

Curved pieces can be easily distorted with an iron, so finger-press your seams first, and then use your iron to press the finished block.

Review Project
Scrappy Circles Baby Quilt

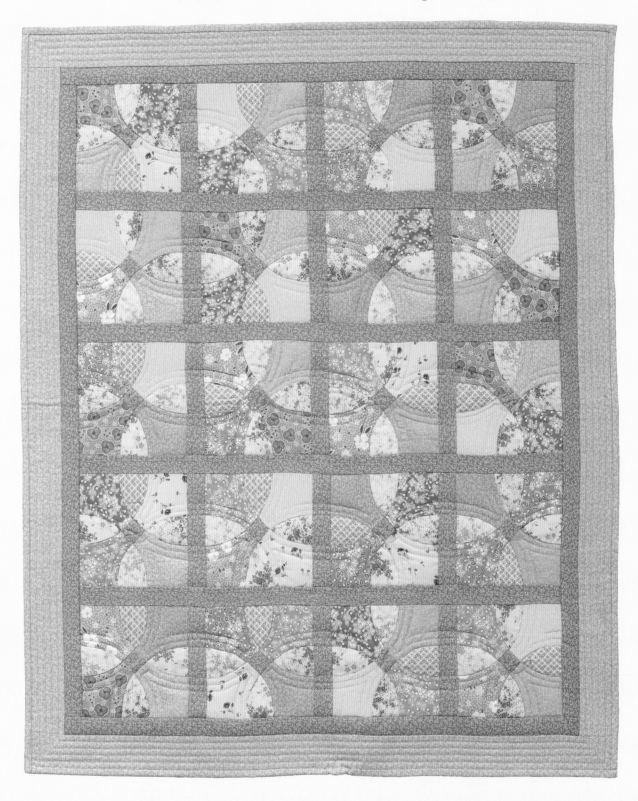

Pieced by Myra Harder and Cori Derksen. Quilted by Myra Harder.

Now that you know the basics of sewing curves, you're ready to practice your new skills on this scrappy quilt. Use a variety of '30s prints for an old-fashioned feel, or change the colors to suit your style.

Finished quilt size: 33" x 40"
Finished block size: 6" x 6"

Materials

Yardage is based on 42"-wide fabric, and we've assumed you'll have 40" of usable width after prewashing and trimming selvages. The yardage requirements allow a 10% cushion for shrinkage and for cutting errors.

⅛ yard *each* of 10 assorted medium prints for template B pieces

⅝ yard of dark pink print for template B pieces, sashing, and inner border

⅛ yard *each* of 4 assorted light prints for template C pieces

⅓ yard of medium print for outer border

⅜ yard of fabric for binding

1⅜ yards of fabric for backing

37" x 44" piece of batting

Cutting

All measurements include ¼"-wide seam allowances. Before you begin cutting, use the A, B, and C patterns on page 21 to make templates from template plastic. Place each template on the right side of the appropriate fabric and use a sharp pencil to draw around it the number of times needed. Cut out the shapes with a scissor.

From the dark pink print, cut:
3 strips, 1½" x width of fabric; crosscut the strips into 15 strips, 1½" x 6½"
2 strips, 1½" x 29½"
4 strips, 1½" x 27½"
2 strips, 1½" x 34½"
20 template B pieces

From the 10 assorted medium prints, cut a *total* of:
80 template A pieces

From the 4 assorted light prints, cut a *total* of:
80 template C pieces

From the outer-border fabric, cut:
2 strips, 2½" x 36½"
2 strips, 2½" x 33½"

From the binding fabric, cut:
4 strips, 2½" x width of fabric

Making the Blocks

Choose a different fabric for each piece in the block.

1. Join one B piece and two A pieces together as shown. Finger-press the seams toward the A pieces. Make 20.

Make 20.

2. Sew a C piece to each side of an A piece as shown. Finger-press the seams toward the A piece. Make 40.

Make 40.

3. Pin a unit from step 2 to one curved edge of a unit from step 1, placing pins at the seam intersections and ends. Stitch the pieces together, gently easing in the fabric as you sew around the curve. Finger-press the seam toward the step 2 unit. Repeat to complete the block. Make 20. Use an iron to press the finished blocks.

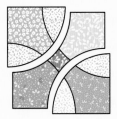 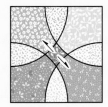

Make 20.

Assembling the Quilt Top

1. Join four blocks and three dark pink print 1½" x 6½" strips together as shown to make a block row. Press the seams toward the dark pink print strips. Make five rows.

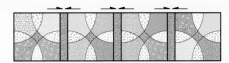

Make 5.

2. Sew the block rows and dark pink print 1½" x 27½" strips together as shown.

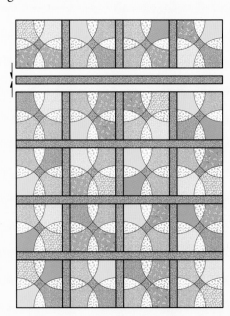

3. Refer to "Adding Borders" on page 60 to sew the dark pink print 1½" x 34½" strips to the sides of the quilt top first; then sew the dark pink print 1½" x 29½" strips to the top and bottom edges. Sew the medium print 2½" x 36½" strips to the sides of the quilt top; then stitch the medium print 2½" x 33½" strips to the top and bottom edges.

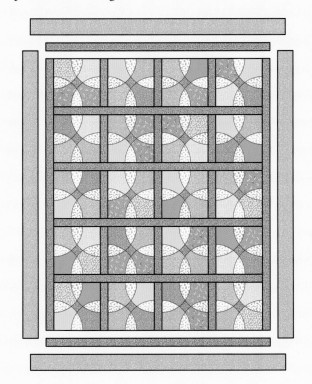

Finishing the Quilt

For detailed instructions on finishing techniques, refer to "Finishing Techniques" on page 60.

1. Cut and piece the backing fabric so that it is 4" to 6" larger than the quilt top. Layer the quilt top with batting and backing. Baste the layers together.

2. Hand or machine quilt as desired.

3. Prepare and sew the binding to the quilt.

4. Block the quilt to square it up.

QUILTING SUGGESTIONS

We wanted to accentuate the curves of the blocks, so we followed the seam lines and quilted over the sashing to join the curves from one block to another. We then echoed these curves by stitching close to the previous lines. That's when the curves really began to show. We finished the outer border with simple lines going around the quilt every ¼". The quilting was kept simple so that it wouldn't detract from the fabrics.

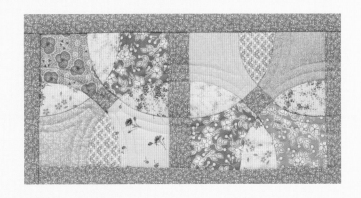

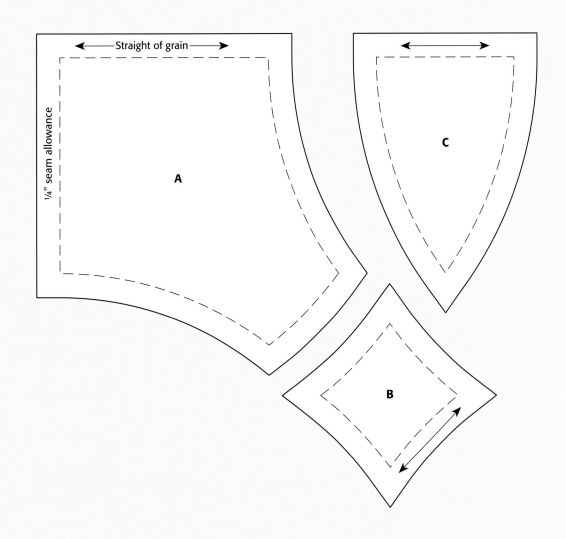

Lesson Three
Technique: *Paper Piecing*

PAPER PIECING IS a good technique to use when you have intricate piecing, sharp points, or unusual shapes and sizes. The pattern is transferred to a paper foundation, and then you place the fabrics on the foundation in numerical order, sew on the pattern lines, and your blocks will come out perfectly. We recommend using one of the papers designed specifically for paper piecing, but you can use any paper that is easy to see through and tear away.

Paper-pieced blocks can begin as single units or multiple units. Single-unit blocks require only one paper-pieced unit to complete the block. Multiple-unit blocks require that more than one separate paper-pieced unit be stitched together to complete the block. The Pinwheel block for the "Blessed Home Sampler Quilt" is a multiple-unit block.

1. Transfer the paper-piecing pattern onto your paper foundation. The easiest way to do this is to photocopy it. Hold the copy up to the light to compare it with your original to make sure no distortion has occurred. You can also trace the pattern onto the foundation material. Use a fine-tip permanent pen or marker and a ruler to trace the lines. Be sure to transfer the numbers that relate to the piecing sequence. The pattern is a mirror image of the finished block.

2. Cut out single-unit block patterns along the dark solid line that runs around the pattern's outer edges. Cut multiple-unit block patterns apart along each dark solid line. Keep in mind that the pattern as it is given in this book is the finished size of the block, so the

fabric pieces need to extend at least ¼" beyond the edges of the unit(s) for the seam allowance.

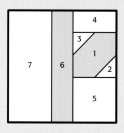 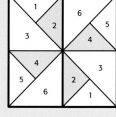

Single-unit block   Multiple-unit block

3. Set the stitch length on your sewing machine for 15 to 18 stitches per inch. Insert a 90/14 needle into the machine. If the paper tears away as you sew, decrease the number of stitches per inch; if the stitches loosen up as you pull the paper foundation away, increase the number of stitches per inch. It isn't necessary to backstitch because the closeness of the stitches keeps the pieces from pulling apart.

4. Place the pattern in front of you with the marked side facing up. This will be referred to as the pattern right side. The unmarked side will be referred to as the wrong side.

5. Cut a piece of fabric for the pattern part marked 1. Be sure it is at least ¼" larger all the way around than the size of the part it will cover. Don't attempt to cut the fabric to size. Just be sure the fabric amply covers the part; all of the excess will be trimmed away later.

6. Hold the pattern up to a light source, with the printed side facing you. Place the wrong side of the fabric piece on the wrong side of the pattern so it covers part 1. Temporarily pin the piece in place. When you hold the block up to the light, part 1 should be completely covered by the fabric with at least ¼" all around for the seam allowances.

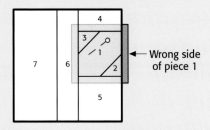
← Wrong side of piece 1

7. Cut a piece of fabric for part 2. The fabric should be at least ¼" larger all the way around.

8. Hold the unit up to a light source, with the right side of the pattern facing you. Place fabric piece 2 over fabric piece 1, right sides together, with at least ¼" of fabric extending over the line that separates parts 1 and 2.

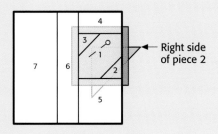
← Right side of piece 2

9. Working on the right side of the pattern, sew along the thin black line that separates parts 1 and 2.

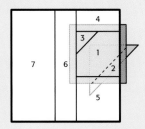

10. Fold back piece 2 along the seam line. Hold the unit up to the light. Be sure that parts 1 and 2 are covered and that the fabric piece for each part extends at least ¼" on all sides.

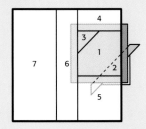

11. Working on the pattern's wrong side, fold piece 2 back down so that the fabric wrong side is facing up. Trim the seam allowance between parts 1 and 2 to ¼". If the excess fabric isn't trimmed away, it can build up and make quilting difficult later.

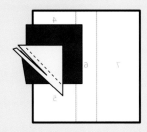

12. Fold piece 2 open. Finger-press or use a wooden pressing tool to press the seam allowance flat.

13. Continue adding fabric pieces, in numerical order, in the same manner for the remaining parts.

14. When you have added all of the fabric pieces to each block or unit, lightly press it and trim the outer seam allowances to ¼".

15. If you are piecing a multiple-unit block, stitch the units together so that they are a mirror image of the block pattern. Lightly press the block.

16. Remove the paper foundation as instructed for each project.

HELPFUL HINTS

The following are just a few paper-piecing hints that we've picked up along the way. We hope they make paper piecing more enjoyable for you.

- *Keep all threads trimmed short so that they don't get caught in your machine and jam things up.*
- *If you use regular photocopy paper as a foundation, lightly mist the paper with water before tearing it off. This makes the paper easier to remove and less likely to rip out your stitches.*
- *Always cut the largest pieces of fabric for your quilt first; then cut up the remaining fabric for paper piecing.*
- *Insert a pin along your intended sewing line on the front side of the pattern. Then when you turn your pattern over to lay down the next piece of fabric, you'll have a seam-allowance guide to assist you in positioning the fabric.*

Review Project
Posy Pots Wall Hanging

Pieced and quilted by Myra Harder

Hang this fresh project on your porch or in your home's entryway during the summer season. It will bring a little bit of the outside in, even on rainy days.

Finished quilt size: 24" x 24"
Finished block size: 4" x 4"

Materials

Yardage is based on 42"-wide fabric, and we've assumed you'll have 40" of usable width after prewashing and trimming selvages. The yardage requirements allow a 10% cushion for shrinkage and for cutting errors.

½ yard of medium green fabric for middle border and outer-border background

⅓ yard of dark green fabric for outer-border vine and leaves

¼ yard of light green fabric for background

⅛ yard of yellow fabric for flower centers and inner border

⅛ yard of plum fabric for flowerpots (we used the reverse of the plum print fabric that was used for the pot rim)

⅛ yard of dark pink fabric for dark flowers

Scraps of light pink fabric for light flower

Scraps of plum print for pot rim

⅜ yard of fabric for binding

⅞ yard of fabric for backing

28" x 28" piece of batting

Cutting

After you finish cutting the following pieces, set the remaining fabrics aside for use while paper piecing. All measurements include ¼"-wide seam allowances.

From the light green, cut:
4 squares, 4½" x 4½"

From the yellow, cut:
2 strips, 1" x 17½"
2 strips, 1" x 16½"

From the medium green, cut:
2 strips, 1" x 18½"
2 strips, 1" x 17½"

From the binding fabric, cut:
3 strips, 2½" x width of fabric

Paper Piecing the Blocks

1. Using the patterns on pages 27–29, transfer 4 Flower blocks, 4 Flowerpot blocks, 2 Large Right Leaf blocks, 2 Large Left Leaf blocks, 12 Small Right Leaf blocks, 12 Small Left Leaf blocks, and 4 Corner blocks to foundation paper.

2. Paper piece the blocks using the fabrics shown.

Dark pink
Flower block.
Make 3.

Light pink
Flower block.
Make 1.

Flowerpot block.
Make 4.

Large Right
Leaf block.
Make 2.

Large Left
Leaf block.
Make 2.

Small Right
Leaf block.
Make 12.

Small Left
Leaf block.
Make 12.

Corner block.
Make 4.

Assembling the Quilt Top

1. Arrange the paper-pieced blocks and the light green 4½" squares into four vertical rows as shown. Sew the pieces in each row together. Sew the rows together.

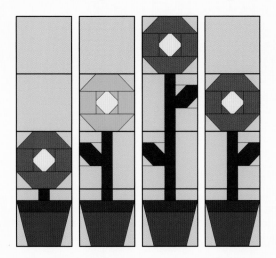

2. Refer to "Adding Borders" on page 60 to sew the yellow 1" x 16½" strips to the sides of the quilt top first; then sew the yellow 1" x 17½" strips to the top and bottom edges. Sew the medium green 1" x 17½" strips to the sides of the quilt top; then stitch the medium green 1" x 18½" strips to the top and bottom edges.

3. Join three Small Right Leaf blocks and three Small Left Leaf blocks as shown to form an outer-border strip. Make four border strips.

Outer border.
Make 4.

4. Refer to the assembly diagram (above right) to sew an outer-border strip to the sides of the quilt top. Sew a corner block to the ends of each of the remaining two border strips; then sew the strips to the top and bottom edges. Be sure the strips are oriented in the correct direction before attaching them to the quilt top.

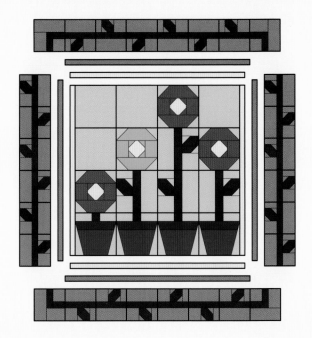

Finishing the Quilt

For detailed instructions on finishing techniques, refer to "Finishing Techniques" on page 60.

1. Cut and piece the backing fabric so that it is 4" to 6" larger than the quilt top. Layer the quilt top with batting and backing. Baste the layers together.

2. Hand or machine quilt as desired.

3. Prepare and sew the binding to the quilt.

4. Block the quilt to square it up.

QUILTING SUGGESTIONS

Because this project is paper pieced, it can be very difficult to hand quilt. We chose to machine quilt the background with vertical rows spaced ¼" apart. We also echo quilted ¼" away from each flower and around the leaves in the outer border.

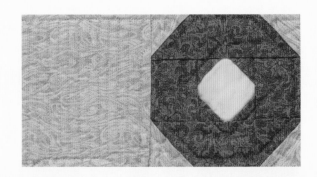

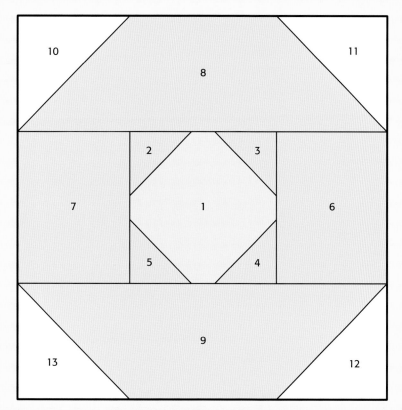

Flower block paper-piecing pattern

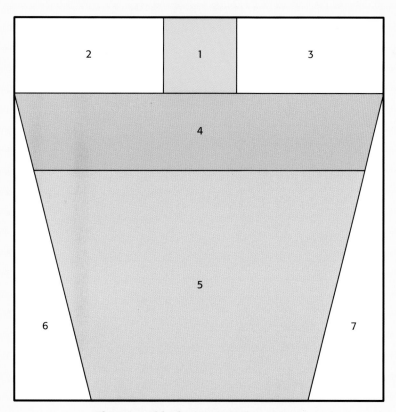

Flowerpot block paper-piecing pattern

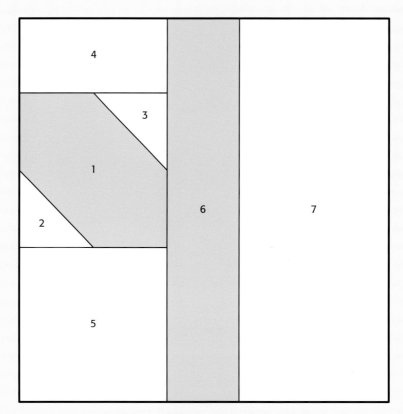

Large Right Leaf block paper-piecing pattern

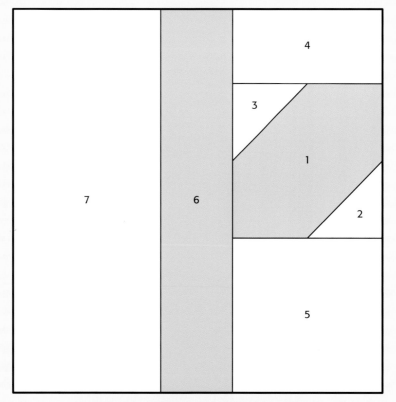

Large Left Leaf block paper-piecing pattern

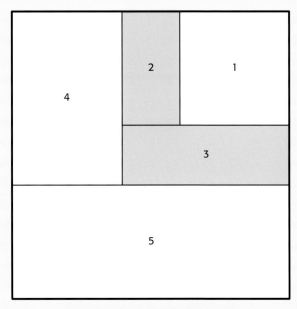

Corner block paper-piecing pattern

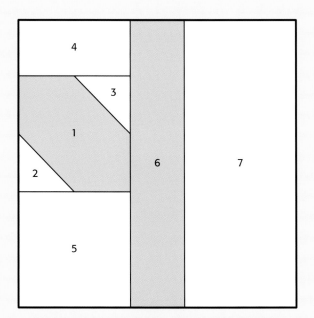

Small Right Leaf block paper-piecing pattern

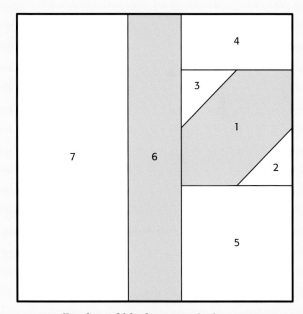

Small Left Leaf block paper-piecing pattern

Lesson Four
Technique: *Hand Appliqué*

MANY OF THE most beautiful quilts are appliquéd or contain appliquéd elements. This technique allows endless possibilities for the designs you can create on your quilts. However, many people are intimidated by the handwork and feel that appliqué is too time consuming. No need! We enjoy preparing the appliqué motifs and then stitching them to the background while watching TV or during long car rides. We've added enough appliqué elements to the sampler quilt that you should have a greater understanding of the technique by the time you have finished. We hope that you'll enjoy appliqué as much as we do and will be able to appreciate appliquéd quilts in a new way.

We use a freezer-paper appliqué method. The method we prefer is to place the freezer paper on the right side of the appliqué fabric, turn the seam allowances under, and stitch down the appliqué. Every new technique takes a little time to get used to, but we feel that once you have practiced this technique a few times, you'll find it as simple and fast as we do. Following are the simple step-by-step instructions for this method.

1. Photocopy the pattern in the book and lay the copied pattern on a light box, or tape it to a window. Place the background fabric over the pattern. Use a sharp pencil to trace the appliqué pattern onto the right side of your background fabric. This gives you an accurate template to follow when placing your appliqué templates on the background blocks. It also ensures that all your blocks are exactly the same.

2. Use a sharp pencil to trace each individual appliqué shape onto the dull side of a piece of freezer paper. Cut out each piece along the traced line. Don't leave any seam allowances around the pieces.

3. Place the freezer-paper pieces on the right side of the appropriate fabrics, shiny side down. Leave approximately ½" between pieces. Press the pieces in place with a hot iron.

4. Cut out each appliqué ¼" from the freezer-paper edges.

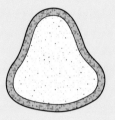

5. Place the appliqué shapes in the appropriate position on the background fabric. If needed, pin each shape in place, pinning through the middle of the piece so that the edges are easily turned under for appliquéing.

6. Turn a portion of the seam allowance under until it's even with the edge of the freezer paper. Using thread that matches the appliqué piece, knot the end of the thread and secure it in the seam allowance. Insert the needle into the background fabric underneath the appliqué piece and come up through the background fabric about ⅛" away. With the tip of the needle, catch just the edge of the appliqué and pull the stitch taut. Continue this process until your piece is completely stitched into place.

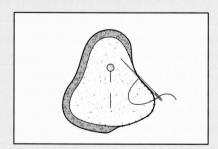

7. Remove the freezer paper.

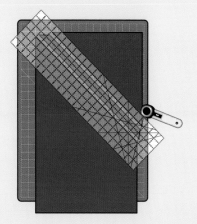

MAKING BIAS TUBES

Bias tubes are often used in appliqué quilts for vines and other curved pieces. No pattern is required for these elements; you simply cut bias strips, stitch them into tubes, and appliqué them in place like any other piece. Bias press bars make the pressing easier, so we recommend investing in a set so that you can make tubes in many different widths.

Following are instructions for making bias tubes.

1. Fold down a corner on the fabric you want to use, forming a triangle. The crosswise grain should meet the lengthwise grain of the fabric. This fold marks the bias and will be the line you'll follow to cut your bias strips.

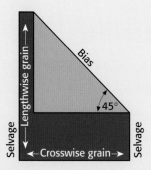

2. Unfold the fabric. Using a ruler and rotary cutter, cut along the diagonal line to make your first cut. Measure from the cut edge and cut bias strips to the width specified in the project instructions as shown above right. Cut strips until you have a little more than the total length needed (above right).

3. If you need a tube that is longer than the length of the cut strip, sew the required amount of strips together as shown.

4. Fold the strip in half lengthwise, wrong sides together. Draw a seam line slightly wider than the width of the bias press bar you will use. This will be the finished width of your bias tube.

5. Stitch along the drawn line and trim the excess seam allowance to ⅛" so that it will be hidden behind the tube after pressing.

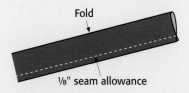

6. Insert the appropriate bias press bar into the tube. Roll the seam allowance to the center of the flat side of the press bar. Press the seam in one direction, slipping the bar through the tube as you continue to press.

7. Remove the press bar and press the tube with a hot iron to hold the crease.

Review Project
Guardian Angels Table Square

Pieced and appliquéd by Cori Derksen. Quilted by Betty Klassen.

This is a great take-along project for your next trip. These easy-to-appliqué elements are fun to do, and by changing the colors to red and green, your topper could easily be transformed into an accent for the holidays.

Finished quilt size: 37½" x 37½"
Finished block size: 16" x 16"

Materials

Yardage is based on 42"-wide fabric, and we've assumed you'll have 40" of usable width after prewashing and trimming selvages. The yardage requirements allow a 10% cushion for shrinkage and for cutting errors.

¾ yard of dark tan print for flowers and fourth border

⅜ yard of dark green fabric for wreath vine and first border

⅜ yard of medium tan fabric for block corner triangles

⅓ yard of light tan fabric for second border

1 fat quarter OR ½ yard of very light tan fabric for block center and angel faces

¼ yard of dark plum fabric for angel dresses, berries, and third border

⅛ yard of gray fabric for angel wings

Scraps of assorted green fabrics for leaves

Scrap of dark brown fabric for angel hair

Scrap of dark red fabric for berries

⅜ yard of fabric for binding

1¼ yards of fabric for backing

42" x 42" piece of batting

Green embroidery floss for flower stems

½"-wide bias press bar

Cutting

All measurements include ¼"-wide seam allowances.

From the very light tan, cut:
1 square, 16½" x 16½"

From the medium tan, cut:
2 squares, 11⅞" x 11⅞"; cut *each* square once diagonally to yield 4 triangles

From the dark green, cut:
2 strips, 1" x 23"
2 strips, 1" x 22"
30" of 1½"-wide bias strips

From the light tan, cut:
2 strips, 2½" x 27"
2 strips, 2½" x 23"

From the dark plum, cut:
2 strips, 1" x 28"
2 strips, 1" x 27"

From the dark tan print, cut:
2 strips, 5½" x 38"
2 strips, 5½" x 28"

Assembling the Table Topper

1. Sew medium tan triangles to opposite sides of the very light tan square. Press the seams toward the triangles. Sew medium tan triangles to the remaining sides of the square; press the seams toward the triangles. Trim the square to 22" x 22", making sure the points of the center square are ¼" from the outer edges.

 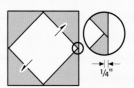

¼"

2. Sew a straight stitch ⅛" from the edges of the square. This will help prevent the edges from raveling as you add the appliqués.

3. Trace the angel appliqué pattern on page 35 onto each corner of the background square made in steps 1 and 2.

4. Fold the square in half vertically and horizontally to mark the center. From the center point measure out 5" in each direction and use a sharp pencil to make a small mark.

5. Refer to "Making Bias Tubes" on page 31 to make the vine from the bias strips. The vine should finish to ½". Place the vine on the background square so that it forms a circle that covers the marks you made in step 4. Cut off any excess so that the ends just meet. Appliqué the vine in place.

6. Use the patterns on page 35 to make 20 leaf, 8 berry, and 4 flower freezer-paper shapes. Also make 4 freezer-paper shapes for each of the 5 angel pieces. Iron the leaf shapes to the assorted green fabrics, the berry shapes to the dark plum and dark red fabrics, and the flower shapes to the dark tan print. For the angel, iron the shapes for pieces 1 and 3 to the dark plum fabric, piece 2 to the very light tan fabric, piece 4 to the gray fabric, and piece 5 to the dark brown fabric. Cut out the shapes ¼" from the freezer-paper edges.

7. Place the leaves on the vine as desired, referring to the photo on page 32 if necessary. Make sure at least one leaf covers the vine ends. Appliqué the shapes in place.

8. Place the berries on and around the vine as desired. Appliqué the shapes in place.

9. Position the angel pieces in place in each corner. Appliqué them in place in numerical order.

10. Refer to the photo to position a flower in front of each angel's hands. Appliqué the shapes in place. Refer to "Technique: Outline-Stitch Embroidery" on page 36 to outline stitch a stem that goes from the flower through each angel's hands.

11. Refer to "Adding Borders" on page 60 to sew the dark green 1" x 22" strips to the sides of the quilt top first; then sew the dark green 1" x 23" strips to the top and bottom edges.

12. Sew the light tan 2½" x 23" strips to the sides of the quilt top; then stitch the light tan 2½" x 27" strips to the top and bottom edges.

13. Sew the dark plum 1" x 27" strips to the sides of the quilt top; then sew the dark plum 1" x 28" strips to the top and bottom edges.

14. Sew the dark tan 5½" x 28" strips to the sides of the quilt top; then sew the 5½" x 38" strips to the top and bottom edges.

Finishing the Table Topper

For detailed instructions on finishing techniques, refer to "Finishing Techniques" on page 60.

1. Cut and piece the backing fabric so that it is 4" to 6" larger than the quilt top. Layer the quilt top with batting and backing. Baste the layers together.

2. Hand or machine quilt as desired.

3. Prepare and sew the binding to the quilt.

4. Block the quilt to square it up.

QUILTING SUGGESTIONS

Several different styles of quilting were used to accent this graceful table square. The quilter, Betty, stipple quilted around the wreath to make the center stand out. She continued to stipple around the angels, using a more open pattern. Simple lines were sewn around the second border, and a more elaborate crisscross of lines was used in the wider fourth border.

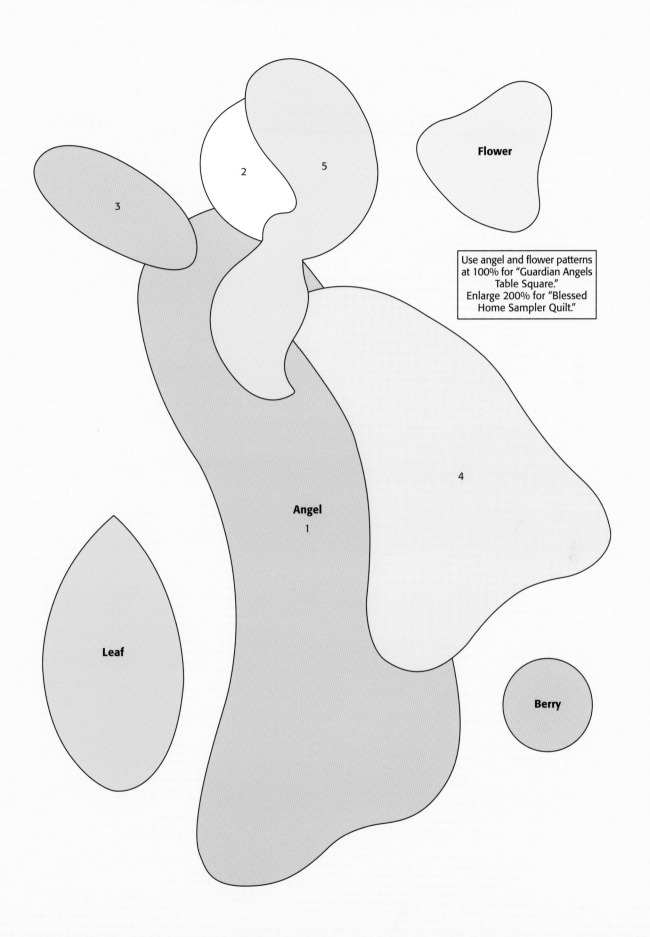

Flower

2

5

3

Use angel and flower patterns at 100% for "Guardian Angels Table Square." Enlarge 200% for "Blessed Home Sampler Quilt."

4

Angel
1

Leaf

Berry

Lesson Five
Technique: *Outline-Stitch Embroidery*

Embellishing quilts with decorative stitches is a practice that has disappeared over time. Because we want to produce quilts quicker and simpler, modern quilters have tended to overlook the details that make many antique quilts so special. The beauty of the old Victorian Crazy quilts is often found in the amazing stitches that are different on each block. We encourage you to look up some of the books that show the many, many beautiful stitches that can simply be done with a few strands of embroidery floss and a needle.

We will introduce you to one stitch in this lesson—the outline stitch. It is one of the easiest and most versatile. As its name implies, it is often used to outline motifs, but it is also used to create details such as tiny stems. For the projects in this book, use a size 22 embroidery needle and the number of floss strands indicated in the instructions. Cut the floss into lengths approximately 18" long to avoid fraying and tangling the floss.

Follow these instructions to make the outline stitch.

1. Thread the needle with two strands of embroidery floss. Knot one end of the floss. Bring the needle up through the fabric at point A and pull the thread taut. Insert the needle at point B and bring it up at point C, pulling the thread taut.

2. Insert the needle at point D, and continue stitching in this manner until you reach the end of your design line. You will work the stitch from left to right.

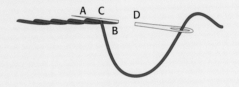

Review Project
Angels Are among Us Pillow

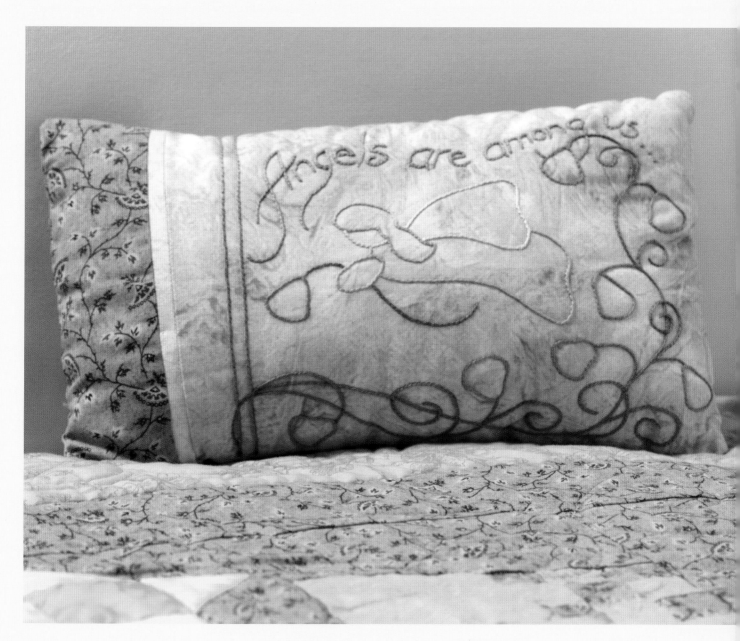

Made by Myra Harder

This pillow is a fun project for all ages. A young girl could complete this project with some supervision. This makes a great gift for a housewarming party, a sick friend, or a special someone's birthday.

Finished pillow size: 11¾" x 7"

Materials

Yardage is based on 42"-wide fabric, and we've assumed you'll have 40" of usable width after prewashing and trimming selvages. The yardage requirements allow a 10% cushion for shrinkage and for cutting errors.

¼ yard of light blue fabric for embroidery background
⅛ yard of medium blue fabric for pillow end
Scrap of light tan fabric for accent strip
Embroidery floss in various colors
Size 22 embroidery needle
Pillow stuffing

Cutting

All measurements include ¼"-wide seam allowances.

From the light blue, cut:
2 rectangles, 7½" x 10"

From the medium blue, cut:
2 rectangles, 2½" x 7½"

From the light tan, cut:
2 rectangles, ¾" x 7½"

Assembling the Pillow

1. Sew one light blue, medium blue, and light tan rectangle together as shown for the pillow front. Repeat to make the pillow back.

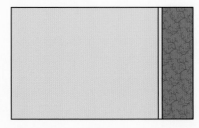

Make 2.

2. Trace the pattern on page 39 onto the light blue rectangle of the front piece. Using six strands of floss and the outline stitch, embroider the words, angel, flowers, and vines. Use a variety of floss colors. Use two strands of floss to make French knots for the dots that follow the words.

French knot

3. Place the pillow back over the front, right sides together. Using a ¼" seam allowance, stitch around the pillow top edges, leaving a 4" opening for turning. Clip the corners and turn the pillow to the right side.

4. Stuff the pillow with stuffing until it is the desired firmness. Slip-stitch the opening closed.

Embroidery pattern

Blessed Home Sampler Quilt

Pieced by Myra Harder and appliquéd by Betty Klassen. Quilted by Jacqueline Pohl.

This sampler has a soft quality with charming and sweet character. Personalize it by using colors that mirror your own home and yard and by adding your family name to the mailbox. It will truly be one of a kind!

READ THIS BEFORE YOU GO TO THE FABRIC STORE!

We've broken the fabrics into two categories: main fabrics and accent fabrics. The main fabrics are used in the sky, ground, house, and border. These are the fabrics that need to work well together to give the quilt the look you want. The sky fabrics should gradually shade from dark at the top to lightest near the ground. The ground fabrics should gradually become darker as they progress from the skyline to the border.

After you've selected the sky and ground fabrics, use the "two steps back" rule to help you determine if you've made the right choices. Lay the fabrics across a table in the order they'll appear in the finished quilt. Place the other main fabrics around them. Now take two big steps back. Does any one print jump out from the others? Sometimes it even helps to walk away for a few minutes, look at something else, and then come back and look at your choices again. If a fabric is wrong, it will jump out at you right away.

The accent fabrics are the smaller pieces of fabrics that are needed for the flowers, windows, stems, and vines. You'll want to make sure that these fabrics work with the main fabrics, but don't sweat over these as much. Choosing a wrong fabric here won't change the overall look of the finished quilt.

Don't choose fabrics that are strongly directional. Because the pieces will be cut up and assembled in many different directions, your fabric will be more efficient if it isn't directional.

Materials and Placement Charts

Yardage is based on 42"-wide fabric, and we've assumed you'll have 40" of usable width after prewashing and trimming selvages. The yardage requirements allow a 10% cushion for shrinkage and for cutting errors.

MAIN FABRICS

Fabric		Yardage	Placement	Notes
	Dark blue	1 yard	Sky	Consider using a small-scale print, rather than a solid, for added interest.
	Light blue	1 yard	Sky	Select a blue that blends well with the dark blue and very light blue.
	Very light blue	1 yard	Sky	This fabric surrounds the house and touches the ground.
	Medium blue	½ yard	Ground (closest to sky), angel's dress	This fabric should blend well with the sky.
	Medium bluish green	⅜ yard	Ground (second from sky)	This fabric should blend with the medium blue and the medium green.
	Medium green	⅓ yard	Ground (third from sky), vine on house	
	Medium-dark green	⅝ yard	Ground (under house)	
	Dark green	½ yard	Ground (under medium-dark green)	
	Very dark green	⅜ yard	Ground (under left side of fence), stems and leaves of curved flowers	
	Light green	2⅝ yards	Outer border, stem for flower in angel's hand, binding	Choose after you've selected sky and ground fabrics. The color you select will determine the overall color of the quilt.
	Cream	1 yard	House, angel wings	Avoid medium-value colors so that the house does not blend into the background.
	Brown	⅔ yard	Large part of roof, window box	
	Dark brown	⅓ yard	Roof trim	
	Medium pink	½ yard	Wide border that runs down left side of quilt	Choose a subtle fabric that doesn't overtake the quilt.
	Dark pink	¼ yard	Narrow border next to medium pink border	This fabric should be about two shades darker than the medium pink fabric.

Fabric		Yardage	Placement	Notes
	Very light green	¼ yard	Sky, ground, windows	
	Tan	¼ yard	Shutters, mailbox, angel's hair	Choose a warm color that isn't too dark or the embroidery on your mailbox will not show.
	Yellow	¼ yard	Friendship Star blocks	Use a soft yellow or the stars will stand out too much.
	Orange	⅛ yard	Friendship Star blocks	This fabric should not contrast too much with the yellow.
	White	⅓ yard	Fence, angel's face	Choose a fabric that stands out against the ground fabrics but isn't too stark. Consider a very dark brown as an alternative.
	Medium red	⅛ yard	Curved flowers	
	Very dark blue	⅛ yard	Ground	
	Medium peach	2" x 24" piece	Window-box flowers	
	Dark green	⅓ yard	Outer-border vine	Color needs to stand out on the outer border. It can be the same or different than one of the darker green ground fabrics.
	Light peach	4" x 4" piece	Flower in angel's hand	
	Dark red	3" x 6" piece	Mailbox flag	
Backing fabric		7¾ yards		
Batting		90" x 102" piece		
Embroidery floss	Brown, dark brown, medium green, dark green		Name and date on mailbox, stems for window-box flowers, windowpane outline	
Paper-piecing paper				
Template plastic				
¼" and ½" bias press bars				

Cutting

All measurements include ¼"-wide seam allowances. Before you cut the following pieces, cut out the irregular shapes found on page 46. Then use patterns A–E on page 56 to make templates from template plastic. To cut the pieces, place each template on the right side of the appropriate fabric and use a sharp pencil to draw around it the number of times needed. Cut out the shapes with scissors.

From the dark blue fabric, cut:

3 strips, 2½" x width of fabric

3 strips, 1½" x width of fabric

1 strip, 2⅞" x width of fabric; crosscut the strip into 10 squares, 2⅞" x 2⅞". Cut each square once diagonally to yield 20 triangles.

2 strips, 2½" x width of fabric; crosscut the strips into 20 squares, 2½" x 2½"

1 rectangle, 6½" x 9½"

1 rectangle, 3½" x 23"

1 rectangle, 3½" x 12½"

2 rectangles, 3½" x 9½"

From the light blue fabric, cut:

3 strips, 2½" x width of fabric

3 strips, 1½" x width of fabric

1 rectangle, 8" x 3½"

3 rectangles, 6½" x 3½"

1 rectangle, 5" x 6½"

1 rectangle, 5" x 3½"

2 rectangles, 3½" x 9½"

1 square, 3½" x 3½"

4 squares, 2⅞" x 2⅞"; cut each square once diagonally to yield 8 triangles

8 squares, 2½" x 2½"

From the very light blue fabric, cut:

1 rectangle, 9½" x 30½"

1 rectangle, 6½" x 15½"

1 rectangle, 6½" x 12½"

1 rectangle, 6½" x 9½"

1 square, 3⅞" x 3⅞"; cut the square once diagonally to yield 2 triangles. You will use 1 and have 1 left over.

1 rectangle, 3½" x 9½"

1 rectangle, 3½" x 6½"

2 squares, 3½" x 3½"

2 squares, 2⅞" x 2⅞"; cut each square once diagonally to yield 4 triangles

4 squares, 2½" x 2½"

2 rectangles, 2" x 6½"

From the medium blue fabric, cut:

2 squares, 6½" x 6½"

1 rectangle, 5" x 6½"

2 squares, 3⅞" x 3⅞"; cut each square once diagonally to yield 4 triangles. You will use 3 and have 1 left over.

2 squares, 3½" x 3½"

2 squares, 2⅞" x 2⅞"; cut each square once diagonally to yield 4 triangles

4 squares, 2½" x 2½"

1 rectangle, 2" x 3½"

From the medium bluish green fabric, cut:

2 squares, 6½" x 6½"

1 rectangle, 5" x 9½"

2 squares, 3⅞" x 3⅞"; cut each square once diagonally to yield 4 triangles

1 rectangle, 3½" x 6½"

1 square, 3½" x 3½"

From the medium green fabric, cut:

1 square, 6½" x 6½"

1 square, 3⅞" x 3⅞"; cut the square once diagonally to yield 2 triangles

1 rectangle, 3½" x 11"

1 rectangle, 3½" x 8"

2 squares, 3½" x 3½"

2 template B pieces

From the medium-dark green fabric, cut:

1 rectangle, 10" x 3½"

1 rectangle, 6½" x 9½"

2 squares, 6½" x 6½"

2 squares, 3⅞" x 3⅞"; cut each square once diagonally to yield 4 triangles. You will use 3 and have 1 left over.

5 squares, 3½" x 3½"

1 rectangle, 2½" x 3½"

1 rectangle, 2" x 5½"

1 rectangle, 2" x 3"

1 rectangle, 2" x 2½"

1 rectangle, 1½" x 7"

1 rectangle, 1½" x 3½"

1 rectangle, 1½" x 2"

3 template B pieces

1 template D piece

1 template E piece

From the dark green fabric, cut:
1 rectangle, 6½" x 18½"
1 rectangle, 6½" x 9½"
1 rectangle, 5½" x 3½"
2 squares, 3⅞" x 3⅞"; cut each
    square once diagonally to yield
    4 triangles
1 rectangle, 3½" x 9½"
3 rectangles, 3½" x 6½"
2 squares, 3½" x 3½"
1 rectangle, 3½" x 2½"
2 rectangles, 2" x 5½"
2 rectangles, 2" x 2½"
1 template B piece
3 template D pieces
2 template E pieces

**From the very dark green fabric,
cut:**
1 square, 3⅞" x 3⅞"; cut the
    square once diagonally to yield
    2 triangles. You will use 1 and
    have 1 left over.
1 rectangle, 3½" x 18½"
1 rectangle, 3½" x 15½"

From the light green fabric, cut:
2 strips, 10" x 78½", along the
    lengthwise grain
2 strips, 10" x 85½", along the
    lengthwise grain

From the cream fabric, cut:
1 rectangle, 15½" x 18½"
1 square, 3⅞" x 3⅞"; cut the
    square once diagonally to yield
    2 triangles
1 square, 3½" x 3½"
2 rectangles, 3½" x 11½"
1 rectangle, 3½" x 6½"
2 rectangles, 2½" x 18½"
2 rectangles, 2" x 6½"
4 rectangles, 2" x 3½"
3 template B pieces
1 template D piece
1 template E piece

From the brown fabric, cut:
1 rectangle, 7½" x 17½"
1 rectangle, 6½" x 9½"
1 rectangle, 5½" x 17½"
1 rectangle, 5½" x 9½"
1 square, 3⅞" x 3⅞"; cut the
    square once diagonally to yield
    2 triangles
1 rectangle, 3½" x 12½"
1 template D piece
1 template E piece

From the dark brown fabric, cut:
2 strips, 3½" x width of fabric
1 strip, 2½" x width of fabric

**From the medium pink fabric,
cut:**
2 strips, 6½" x width of fabric
1 rectangle, 6½" x 9½"
1 rectangle, 3½" x 6½"
1 rectangle, 2" x 5½"
1 rectangle, 2" x 2½"
2 template D pieces
1 template E piece

From the dark pink fabric, cut:
1 rectangle, 2" x 21½"
1 rectangle, 2" x 18½"
1 rectangle, 2" x 6½"
2 rectangles, 2" x 3½"
1 template E piece

**From the very light green fabric,
cut:**
1 rectangle, 6½" x 11½"
1 square, 3½" x 3½"

From the tan fabric, cut:
1 rectangle, 5½" x 9½"
2 rectangles, 3½" x 11½"

From the yellow fabric, cut:
2 strips, 2⅞" x width of fabric;
    crosscut the strips into 18
    squares, 2⅞" x 2⅞". Cut each
    square once diagonally to yield
    36 triangles.

From the orange fabric, cut:
9 squares, 2½" x 2½"

From the white fabric, cut:
7 rectangles, 3½" x 6½"
1 rectangle, 3½" x 2½"
1 rectangle, 2" x 9½"
5 rectangles, 2" x 2½"
7 template C pieces

From the medium red fabric, cut:
9 template A pieces

**From the very dark blue fabric,
cut:**
1 rectangle, 2" x 5½"
1 rectangle, 2" x 2½"
1 template D piece
2 template E pieces

From the dark red fabric, cut:
1 rectangle, 2" x 3"
1 square, 1½" x 1½"

Cutting the Irregular Shapes

There are three large, irregular shapes in the sampler quilt. They are the center peak of the house, the sky to the left of the peak, and the roof to the right of the peak. You will need to follow the diagrams below to draw the pieces on the right side of the fabric indicated and cut them out. Set these pieces aside.

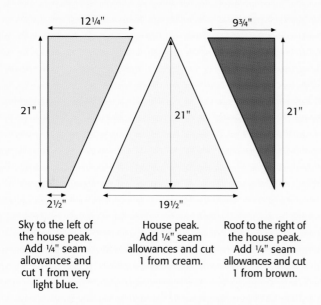

Sky to the left of the house peak. Add ¼" seam allowances and cut 1 from very light blue.

House peak. Add ¼" seam allowances and cut 1 from cream.

Roof to the right of the house peak. Add ¼" seam allowances and cut 1 from brown.

Cutting the Bias Strips and Making the Bias Tubes

There are four places on the quilt where bias tubes are used—the vine on the front of the house, the stems of the curved flowers, the stem of the angel's flower, and the vine on the outer border. Refer to "Technique: Hand Appliqué" on page 30 for specific information on making the bias tubes. The tubes will be constructed now and applied later.

1. For the front of the house, you will need approximately 75" of bias tubes cut from the medium green fabric. Cut your strips 1" wide and finish the tubes so that they are ¼" wide. We did not make one long piece of bias tube for this section. Instead, we made several shorter pieces and curved them into each other. Set the tubes aside for use in unit 9.

2. Cut the bias strips for the stems of the curved flowers from the very dark green fabric. The strips should be cut 1" and finish to ¼" wide. You will need four lengths that are 9" long and five lengths that are 11" long.

3. Cut approximately 12" of 1"-wide bias strip from the light green fabric and make a ¼"-wide finished bias tube for the stem of the angel's flower.

4. The outer-border vine is made from the dark green for vines. Cut the strips 1½" wide and make approximately 115" of continuous bias tube that finishes to ½" wide.

Assembling the Blocks

Six different blocks—Square Nine Patch, Elongated Nine Patch, Friendship Star, Pinwheel, Square-in-a-Square, and Curved Flower—will be needed for the sky and background. The pieces for the Square Nine Patch, Elongated Nine Patch, Friendship Star, and Curved Flower blocks have already been cut. Use leftovers of the appropriate fabrics to construct the paper-pieced Pinwheel and Square-in-a-Square blocks.

NINE PATCH BLOCKS

The two different Nine Patch blocks make up part of the sky. They are both made the same way but are different sizes. Refer to "Technique: Strip Piecing" on page 12 for specific information on making strip sets.

1. Use the dark blue and light blue 1½"-wide strips to make strip sets as shown. Crosscut each strip set into the number of 1½"-wide segments indicated.

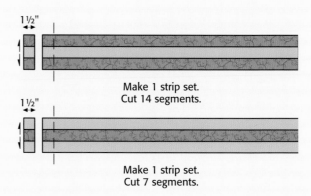

Make 1 strip set.
Cut 14 segments.

Make 1 strip set.
Cut 7 segments.

2. Join three segments as shown to make a Square Nine Patch block. Make 7.

Square Nine Patch block.
Make 7.

3. Use the dark blue and light blue 2½"-wide strips to make strip sets as shown. Crosscut each strip set into the number of 3½"-wide segments indicated.

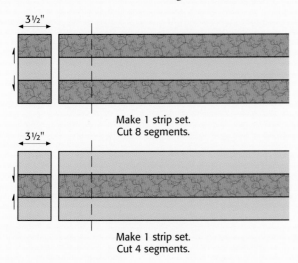

Make 1 strip set.
Cut 8 segments.

Make 1 strip set.
Cut 4 segments.

4. Join three segments as shown to make an Elongated Nine Patch block. Make four.

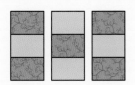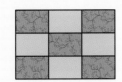

Elongated Nine Patch block.
Make 4.

FRIENDSHIP STAR BLOCKS

There are nine Friendship Star blocks in the sky section. They are each made the same but have different background colors.

1. Join a yellow 2⅞" triangle to each dark blue, light blue, very light blue, and medium blue 2⅞" triangle along the long edges as shown to make a square. Make the number shown for each combination.

Make 20.   Make 8.   Make 4.   Make 4.

2. Arrange four dark blue/yellow squares from step 1, four dark blue 2½" squares, and one orange 2½" square into three horizontal rows as shown. Sew the units in each row together, and then sew the rows together to complete the block. Make five. Repeat to make the remaining blocks, using the squares from step 1 and the light blue, very light blue, medium blue, and orange 2½" squares. The blue squares in each block should match the blue used in the step 1 squares.

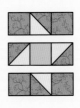

Friendship Star block.
Make 5.

Make 2.   Make 1.   Make 1.

PINWHEEL BLOCKS

Refer to "Technique: Paper Piecing" on page 22 for specific information on paper piecing.

1. Using the Pinwheel block pattern on page 57, transfer three patterns to paper foundations.

2. Paper piece the units using the fabrics shown. You will use pieces of light blue, very light blue, very light green, and medium blue fabrics. Make two of each unit.

Make 2.   Make 2.   Make 2.

3. Sew two units with the same colors together as shown to complete the blocks.

Pinwheel blocks.
Make 1 of each.

SQUARE-IN-A-SQUARE BLOCKS

Refer to "Technique: Paper Piecing" on page 22 for specific information on paper piecing.

1. Using the Square-in-a-Square block pattern on page 58, transfer four patterns to paper foundations.

2. Paper piece the blocks using the fabrics shown. You will use pieces of very dark green, dark green, medium green, very dark blue, medium blue, very light green, and medium bluish green fabrics.

Square-in-a-Square blocks.
Make 1 of each.

CURVED FLOWER BLOCKS

Refer to "Technique: Curved Piecing" on page 17 to sew each A piece to a B piece to complete the blocks. Set the blocks aside.

Make 3.   Make 3.

Make 2.   Make 1.

Assembling the Fence Sections

1. Refer to the diagram to sew the correct-colored template D pieces to the left side of the white template C pieces and the correct-colored template E pieces to the right side of the white template C pieces. You will use pieces cut from dark green, very dark blue, medium-dark green, medium pink, and dark pink fabrics. Sew a white 3½" x 6½" rectangle to the bottom of each piece.

Make 2.   Make 1.   Make 1.

 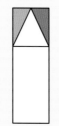 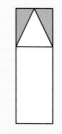
Make 1.   Make 1.   Make 1.

2. To make the left fence section, refer to the diagram to sew the correct-colored 2" x 5½" and 2" x 2½" rectangles to each side of a white 2" x 2½" rectangle to create the sections between the pickets. Sew these sections and the appropriate pickets together in the order shown.

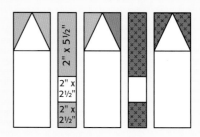

Left fence section

3. To make the right fence section, refer to the diagram to sew the correct-colored pieces together to create the sections between the pickets in the same manner as in step 2. Sew these sections and the appropriate pickets together in the order shown. Add the white 2" x 9½" rectangle to the left side of the section.

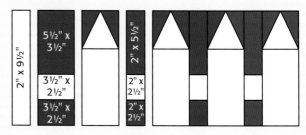

Right fence section

4. Set the fence sections aside.

Assembling the Window Box

1. Sew a cream D piece and a brown D piece together along the long edges to make a rectangle. Sew the cream and brown E pieces together in the same manner.

2. Sew the units to the ends of the brown 3½" x 12½" rectangle as shown.

3. Set the window box aside.

Assembling the Units

The pieces you have cut or made will now be assembled into larger units. Once all of the units have been constructed, we can put them together to make the quilt top and then add the appliquéd elements.

UNIT 1

1. Sew the medium pink 6½" x 9½" rectangle to the top of a Friendship Star block with a dark blue background.

2. Join the two medium pink 6½" x width of fabric strips end to end to make one long strip. From the pieced strip, cut one 6½" x 48½" strip and sew it to the bottom of the Friendship Star block.

UNIT 2

1. To make the top section, sew the dark pink 2" x 3½" rectangle to one end of the dark blue 3½" x 23" rectangle.

2. To make the bottom-left section, join a light blue 6½" x 3½" rectangle to the bottom of a Friendship Star block with a dark blue background. Sew an Elongated Nine Patch block to the left side of this unit.

3. To make the bottom-right section, add the light blue 3½" square to the left side of a Square Nine Patch block. Sew a light blue 6½" x 3½" rectangle to the bottom of this unit. Sew a Friendship Star block with a dark blue background to the right side of the joined unit. Sew a Square Nine Patch block to the right end of a dark blue 3½" x 9½" rectangle and sew this strip to the top of the section.

4. Sew the bottom-left section to the left side of the lower-right section. Add the top section to the top of the joined sections.

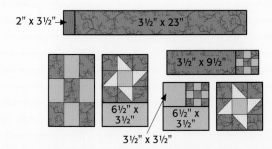

UNIT 3

1. To make the left section, sew a dark blue 3½" x 9½" rectangle to the top of an Elongated Nine Patch block. Sew the very light blue 3½" x 9½" rectangle to the bottom of the Elongated Nine Patch block.

2. To make the top-right section, sew a Square Nine Patch block to the right end of a light blue 3½" x 9½" rectangle. Add a dark blue 3½" x 12½" rectangle to the top of this unit. Join a Friendship Star block with a dark blue background to the right side of this unit. Sew a dark blue 6½" x 9½" rectangle to the right side of the Friendship Star block.

3. To make the bottom-right section, sew the very light blue 6½" x 15½" rectangle to the left side of an Elongated Nine Patch block. Sew a light blue 6½" x 3½" rectangle to the right side of the Elongated Nine Patch block.

4. Sew the top-right section to the top of the lower-right section. Join the left section to the left side of this unit.

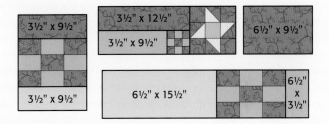

UNIT 4

1. To make the top section, sew a light blue 5" x 3½" rectangle to the left side of a Square Nine Patch block. Join a light blue 8" x 3½" rectangle to the top of this unit. Sew the dark pink 2" x 6½" rectangle to the left side of this unit.

2. To make the bottom section, sew a very light blue 2" x 6½" rectangle to the right side of a Friendship Star block with a light blue background and another one to a Friendship Star block with a very light blue background. Sew a very light blue 3½" square to the bottom of a Square Nine Patch block. Sew the light blue 5" x 6½" rectangle to the left side of this unit. Add the unit with the light blue Friendship Star unit to the top of this unit and the very light blue Friendship Star unit to the bottom of this unit.

Join the dark pink 2" x 18½" rectangle to the left side of the joined units.

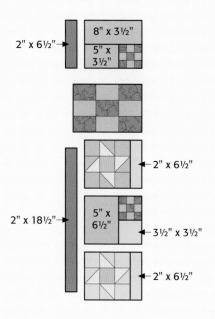

3. Sew the top section to the top of an Elongated Nine Patch block and the bottom section to the bottom of the Elongated Nine Patch block.

UNIT 5

1. To make the left section, sew a very light blue 3½" x 6½" rectangle to the bottom of a Friendship Star block with a light blue background.

2. To make the middle section, join a light blue 3½" x 9½" rectangle to the top of the very light blue 6½" x 9½" rectangle. Sew this unit to the right side of the left section.

3. Sew the very light blue 9½" x 30½" rectangle to the right side of the middle section.

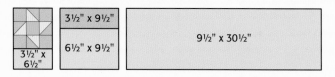

UNIT 6

1. To make the left section, join the three irregular-shaped pieces you cut out earlier (see "Cutting the Irregular Shapes" on page 46) as shown.

2. To make the middle section, sew cream 2" x 3½" rectangles to each side of the very light green 3½" square. Add cream 2" x 6½" rectangles to the top and bottom of this unit. Sew each 3⅞" cream triangle to a brown 3⅞" triangle to make a square. Sew these squares together with the cream triangles facing each other. Sew this unit to the top of the previous unit. Add the brown 5½" x 9½" rectangle to the left side

of the unit and the brown 6½" x 9½" rectangle to the right side of the unit. Join the brown 5½" x 17½" rectangle to the bottom of the unit and the brown 7½" x 17½" rectangle to the top of the unit.

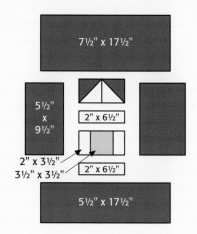

3. To make the right section, sew the very light blue 3⅞" triangle to a medium blue 3⅞" triangle to make a square. Sew a medium blue 3½" square to the left side of the pieced square. Sew a medium blue 6½" square to the bottom of the unit and the very light blue 6½" x 12½" rectangle to the top of the unit.

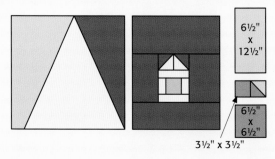

4. Sew the left section to the left side of the middle section. Sew the right section to the right side of the middle section.

UNIT 7

1. To make the top-right section, sew a medium blue 3⅞" triangle to a medium bluish green 3⅞" triangle to make a pieced square. Join the medium bluish green 3½" square to the right side of the pieced square. Add a medium blue 6½" square to the top of this unit and a medium bluish green 6½" square to the bottom of this unit. Sew a medium bluish green 3⅞" triangle to a medium green 3⅞" triangle to make a pieced square. Join a medium green 3½" square to the right side of the pieced square. Sew this unit to the bottom of the previous unit.

2. To make the top-middle section, sew the medium blue 2" x 3½" rectangle to the right side of a Square Nine Patch block. Sew the medium blue 5" x 6½" rectangle to the bottom of this unit. Add the medium bluish green 5" x 9½" rectangle to the bottom of the previous unit.

3. Sew the top-middle section to the left side of the top-right section. Join the medium green 3½" x 11" rectangle to the bottom of the joined sections. Add the dark pink 2" x 21½" rectangle to the left side of these joined sections.

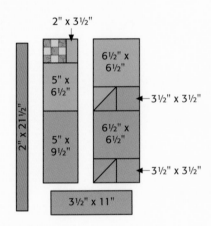

UNIT 8

1. To make the window section, sew tan 3½" x 11½" rectangles to each side of the very light green 6½" x 11½" rectangle. Add cream 3½" x 11½" rectangles to each side of this unit. Sew a cream 2½" x 18½" rectangle to the top of the unit.

2. Sew cream 2" x 3½" rectangles to the ends of the window-box section that you made previously (see page 48). Join a cream 2½" x 18½" rectangle to the bottom of the window-box section. Add this section to the bottom of the window section.

3. Arrange three Curved Flower blocks with cream backgrounds together with the cream 3½" square and the cream 3½" x 6½" rectangle as shown. Be sure the flowers are facing the directions shown. The stems

will be appliquéd in place later. Add this unit to the bottom of the window-box section.

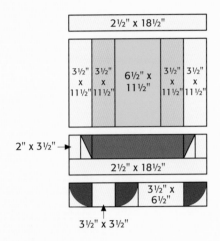

UNIT 9

1. To make the left section, refer to "Technique: Hand Appliqué" on page 30 to arrange and appliqué the medium green ¼" bias tubes on the cream 15½" x 18½" rectangle to resemble vines. Refer to the photo if necessary or use your own design. Sew the medium-dark green 2" x 3" rectangle to the top of the dark red 2" x 3" rectangle. Add a medium-dark green 3½" square to the right side of this unit and the medium-dark green 10" x 3½" rectangle to the left side. Sew this unit to the bottom of the appliquéd unit.

2. To make the top-right section, sew a medium blue 3⅞" triangle to a medium bluish green 3⅞" triangle to make a pieced square. Sew a medium blue 3½" square to the right side of the pieced square. Add the medium bluish green 6½" square to the bottom of this unit. Sew a medium bluish green 3⅞" triangle to a medium green 3⅞" triangle to make a pieced square. Add the medium bluish green 3½" x 6½" rectangle to the top of this pieced square. Sew the unit to the left side of the previous unit.

3. To make the middle-right section, sew a Curved Flower block with a medium green background to the bottom of the medium green 3½" square as shown. Sew the medium green 6½" square to the left side of this unit. The flower stem will be appliquéd in place later.

4. To make the bottom-right section, sew a medium-dark green 3½" square to the bottom of a Curved Flower block with a medium-dark green background.

Add a medium-dark green 6½" square to the right side of this unit. The flower stem will be appliquéd in place later.

5. Sew the top-right section to the top of the middle-right section and the bottom-right section to the bottom of the middle-right section. Be careful not to catch the stems in the seams. Sew the left section to the left side of the right section.

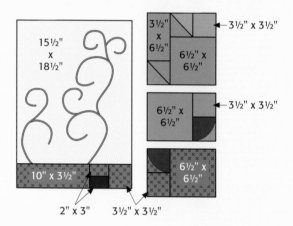

UNIT 10

1. To make the top section, sew a very light blue 3½" square to the left side of a Square Nine Patch block. Sew this unit to the bottom of a Friendship Star block with a dark blue background.

2. To make the middle section, join the three Pinwheel blocks together in the order shown. Sew these to the bottom of the top section.

3. Join the three Square-in-a-Square blocks together as shown. Sew the Friendship Star block with a medium blue background to the top of the unit. Add this strip to the bottom of the middle section.

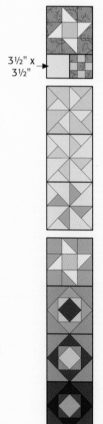

UNIT 11

1. To make the top section, sew the medium pink 3½" x 6½" rectangle to the left side of a dark pink 2" x 3½" rectangle. Sew the medium green 3½" x 8" rectangle to the right side of this unit. Add a Curved Flower block with a medium green background to the end of the strip as shown. The flower stem will be appliquéd in place later.

2. To make the middle-right section, sew the medium-dark green 1½" x 3½" rectangle to the left side of a Curved Flower block with a medium green background as shown. The flower stem will be appliquéd in place later. Sew the medium-dark green 2½" x 3½" rectangle to the right side of the Curved Flower block. Sew a medium-dark green 3⅞" triangle to a dark green 3⅞" triangle to make a pieced square. Sew the pieced square to the right side of a medium-dark green 3½" square. Sew a dark green 3½" x 6½" rectangle to the bottom of this unit.

3. Sew the left fence section that you made previously (see page 48) to the left side of the middle-right section. Sew the very dark green 3½" x 18½" rectangle to the bottom of this unit. Add the top section to the top of this unit.

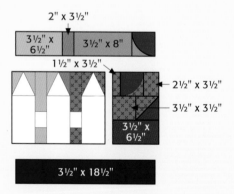

UNIT 12

1. To make the top section, sew a medium-dark green 3½" square to the bottom of a Curved Flower block with a medium-dark green background as shown. Join a medium-dark green 6½" square to the right side of this unit. The flower stem will be appliquéd in place later. Add the medium-dark green 6½" x 9½" rectangle to the left side of this unit.

2. To make the bottom section, sew the very dark green 3⅞" triangle to a dark green 3⅞" triangle to make a pieced square. Add the very dark green 3½" x 15½" rectangle to the left side of the pieced square. Join the dark green 6½" x 18½" rectangle to the top of this unit.

3. Sew the top section to the top of the bottom section.

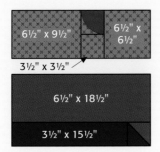

UNIT 13

1. To make the top-left section, sew the medium-dark green 1½" x 2" rectangle to the right side of the dark red 1½" square. Sew the medium-dark green 1½" x 7" rectangle to the left side of this unit. Join the tan 5½" x 9½" rectangle to the bottom of this unit. Sew the medium-dark green 3⅞" triangles to dark green 3⅞" triangles to make two pieced squares. Sew a medium-dark green 3½" square to the top of one pieced square as shown. Sew this unit to the left side of the previous unit. Sew a dark green 3½" square to the bottom of the remaining pieced square as shown. Sew this unit to the right side of the previous unit.

2. To make the top-right section, sew the dark green 6½" x 9½" rectangle to the left side of the remaining Square-in-a-Square block. Sew this section to the right side of the top-left section.

3. To make the bottom-left section, sew a dark green 3½" square to the left side of a Curved Flower block with a dark green background as shown. Sew a dark green 3½" x 6½" rectangle to the bottom of this unit. Add the remaining dark green 3½" x 6½" rectangle to the right side of the unit; then add a dark green 3½" x 9½" rectangle to the top of the unit. Sew this unit to the left side of the right fence section that you made previously (see page 48).

4. Sew the top section to the top of the bottom section.

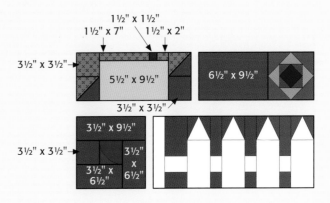

Assembling the Quilt Top

1. Refer to the assembly diagram to join the units as shown.

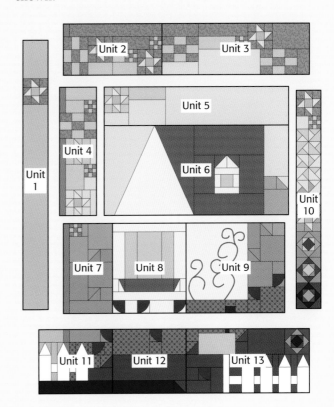

2. Sew the light green 10" x 78½" strips to the sides of the quilt top. Press the seams toward the borders. Sew the light green 10" x 85½" strips to the top and bottom edges. Press the seams toward the borders.

Adding the Appliqué Elements

Refer to "Technique: Hand Appliqué" on page 30.

1. Use the patterns on page 59 to make 1 upper window, 2 upper-window shutter, 7 window-box flower, and 57 leaf freezer-paper shapes. Enlarge the angel and flower patterns on page 39 to 200%. Make one flower freezer-paper shape and one freezer-paper shape for each of the five angel pieces. Iron the upper-window shape to the very light green fabric, the upper-window-shutter shapes to the tan fabric, and the window-box-flower shapes to the medium peach fabric. Iron nine leaf shapes to the very dark green fabric you used for the flower stems. Iron the remaining leaf shapes to the remaining pieces of the green fabrics used for the ground. For the angel, iron the shapes for pieces 1 and 3 to the medium blue fabric, piece 2 to the white fabric, piece 4 to the cream fabric, and piece 5 to the tan fabric. Iron the angel's flower to the light peach fabric. Cut out the shapes ¼" from the freezer-paper edges.

2. On one end of each very dark green bias tube, turn the ends to the inside of the tube about ¼"; press. Refer to the photo on page 40 to position and appliqué the tubes in place for the stems of the curved flowers, placing the turned-under end closest to the flower. Appliqué a very dark green leaf to the bottom of each stem to cover the raw ends.

3. Fold the dark brown 3½"-wide strips in half lengthwise and gently crease the fold. Open up the strips. With the right side up, lay one strip along the left side of the house peak, positioning the creased line on the strip over the seam where the peak and sky are joined. Lay the remaining strip on the right side of the house peak in the same manner. The lower edge of

the strips should extend ¼" beyond the seam joining unit 6 to units 7, 8, and 9. At the peak, overlap the strips; then turn the top strip under to form a point that corresponds to the peak. Lightly crease the fold and cut the excess away from both strips. Place a piece of masking tape on the strips, ¼" away from the raw edges. Use the tape straight edge as a guide to appliqué the edges in place. Remove the masking tape.

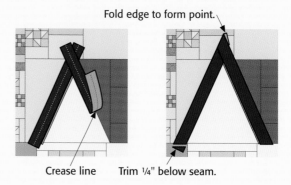

Fold edge to form point.

Crease line   Trim ¼" below seam.

4. Repeat step 3 with the dark brown 2½"-wide strip to add the trim to the small window. Position the inside edges of the trim so that they go along the top corners of the window "glass" and the trim bottom edges are just above the lower edge of the "glass."

5. Arrange the angel shapes in the sky above the house. Appliqué them in place in numerical order. Refer to the photo to position a flower in front of the angel's hand. Appliqué the shape in place. Appliqué the light green bias tube in place to create a stem above and below the angel's hand.

6. Arrange the window-box-flower shapes above the window box as desired and appliqué them in place. You will embroider the stems later.

7. Lay the dark green bias tube along the left side and bottom border, curving the tube as desired to create the main shape. Cut off two pieces to make additional curves at the top and bottom of the vine. Appliqué the vine in place. Position the remaining leaves on the vine as desired and appliqué them in place.

Adding the Embroidered Details

Refer to "Technique: Outline-Stitch Embroidery" on page 36.

1. Use six strands of medium green embroidery floss to outline all of the windows and create the window frame of the bottom window. Be creative with the bottom window frame and make it any way you'd like.

2. Use two strands of dark green and/or dark brown to stitch the stems for the flowers in the window box. You can curve these in any direction you desire.

3. Draw a 5" x 9" rectangle on a blank piece of white paper. Write your family name and the year on the paper. Using a light box or a window, trace your name from the paper onto your mailbox piece. Stitch the name with six strands of dark brown and the year with six strands of brown.

Finishing the Quilt

For detailed instructions on finishing techniques, refer to "Finishing Techniques" on page 60.

1. Cut and piece the backing fabric so that it is 4" to 6" larger than the quilt top. Layer the quilt top with batting and backing. Baste the layers together.

2. Hand or machine quilt as desired.

3. Prepare and sew the binding to the quilt.

4. Block the quilt to square it up.

QUILTING SUGGESTIONS

Jacqueline added a lot of character to this quilt top. In the large amount of open sky, she drew in some large swirls to look like the wind, and ignored where individual blocks started and stopped. By having the swirls overlap the blocks, the sky blends together. The large roof of the house has horizontal lines, like shingles on a roof. Quilting horizontal lines into the shutters and outlining the windowpanes added more detail. Leaves were quilted onto the vines that grow on the side of the house. Each layer of ground has its own design, but the layers all blend together well so that the finished look is very gentle. There will still be areas where it's best to outline the blocks with quilting, called stitching in the ditch. This would work with the Friendship Star blocks and the pieced blocks that run down the right side of the quilt. The wide outer border is a great place to experiment. Make sure that your quilting follows through to the border edges so that the quilt lies flat when you are finished. Jacqueline quilted a very beautiful and unique wide vine in the border, which was the perfect frame for our home.

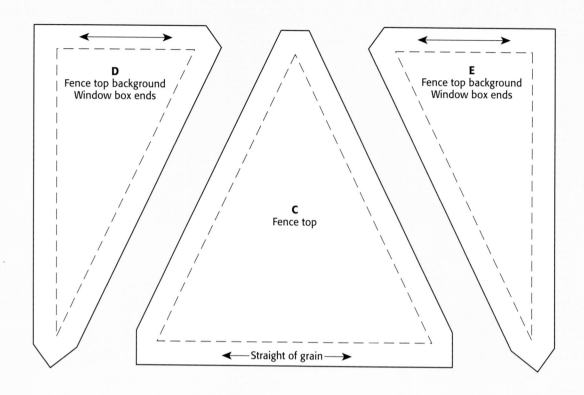

D
Fence top background
Window box ends

C
Fence top

E
Fence top background
Window box ends

←— Straight of grain —→

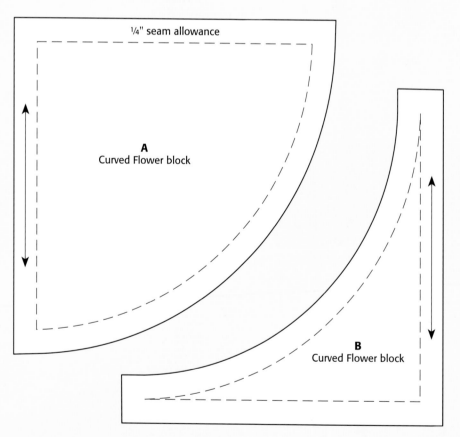

¼" seam allowance

A
Curved Flower block

B
Curved Flower block

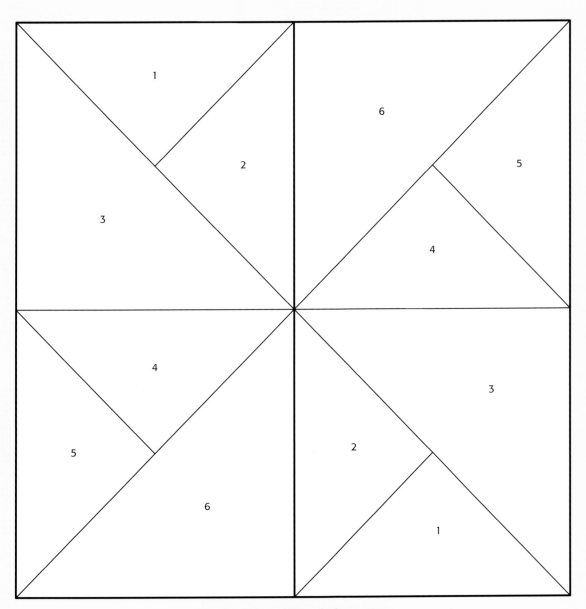

Pinwheel block paper-piecing pattern

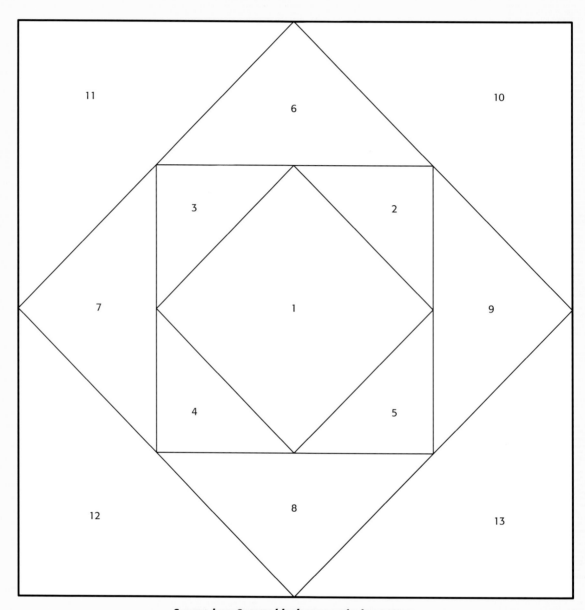

Square-in-a-Square block paper-piecing pattern

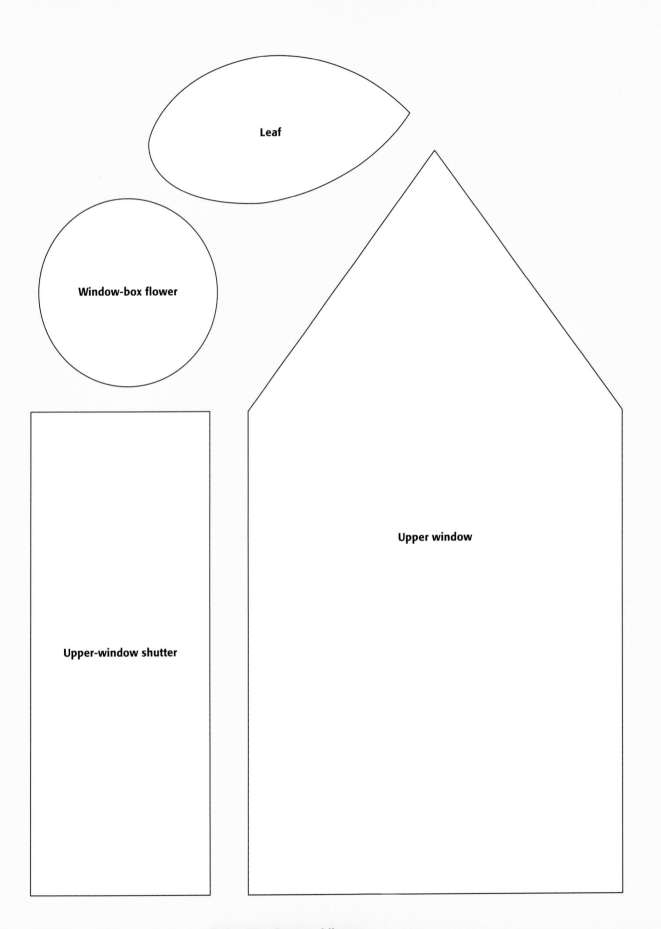

Leaf

Window-box flower

Upper-window shutter

Upper window

We hope you're proud of the projects you've made and are ready to complete the final steps so that you can show them off.

Adding Borders

Although specific border lengths are listed in the cutting instructions for each project, it is best to measure your quilt top through the center in both directions before cutting border strips for your quilt. Cut your border strips across the width of the fabric and piece as necessary unless otherwise indicated. We typically add the side borders first, and then the top and bottom borders as indicated below.

1. Measure the length of your quilt top through the center and cut two border strips to that measurement, piecing as necessary to achieve the needed length. Mark the centers of the strips and the centers along the side edge of the quilt top. Pin the strips to the sides of the quilt, matching the centers and ends. Stitch in place. Press the seam allowances toward the borders.

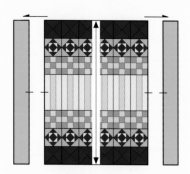

Measure center of
quilt, top to bottom.
Mark centers.

2. Measure the width of your quilt through the center, including the just-added borders, and cut two border strips to that measurement, piecing as necessary.

Mark the centers of the strips and the centers along the top and bottom edges of the quilt top. Pin the strips to the top and bottom edges of the quilt, matching the centers and ends. Stitch in place. Press the seam allowances toward the borders.

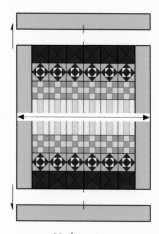

Mark centers.
Measure center of quilt, side to
side, including border strips.

Assembling the Layers

Once the quilt top is finished, you'll need to layer it with the batting and backing before you quilt it.

1. Decide how you are going to quilt your project. You can follow the seams and stitch in the ditch, try freehand quilting, or you could mark your quilt top with a quilting stencil or other design. Most quilters find it easiest to mark the top before layering and basting, so do this first if necessary.

2. Cut the backing and batting 4" to 6" larger than the pieced top. This will give you 2" to 3" extra on each side for the take-up that occurs during quilting. The project instructions in this book will include the size to cut the batting and backing. For backings that are pieced together, you may need to trim some of the excess away before continuing the process.

3. Place the backing, right side down, on a flat surface. Use masking tape to secure it in several places along the edges. Make sure the backing is smooth and taut, but not stretched too tightly. Position the batting over the backing and smooth it into place. Center the pieced top, right side up, over the batting and backing.

4. Working from the center out, baste the layers together with thread or safety pins. Use thread if you plan to hand quilt, or safety pins if you are going to machine quilt. Space the pins or basting stitches 4" to 6" apart.

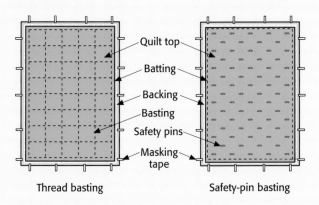

Thread basting   Safety-pin basting

Quilting

Quilting is an important finishing step. Not only does it hold the layers together, but it also enhances the quilt pattern and adds dimension to the project. We love hand quilting because it adds to a quilt's worth—both the monetary value and the heirloom quality as well. Not everyone has the time for or the love of hand quilting, however, so machine quilting is another option. Machine quilting can be faster and allows you to make intricate or repeating patterns easily. Maurine Noble's *Machine Quilting Made Easy!* (Martingale & Company, 1994) is a good resource for learning about machine quilting. Sometimes a combination of hand and machine quilting is also used. For more information on hand quilting, we recommend the book *Loving Stitches: A Guide to Fine Hand Quilting, Revised Edition* by Jeana Kimball (Martingale & Company, 2003).

Adding a Hanging Sleeve

We like to add a hanging sleeve to the back of our projects before we bind them.

1. Cut a strip of fabric that is 6" wide with a length that is 1" less than the width of the finished project.

2. Press under each end of the strip ¼" and stitch in place.

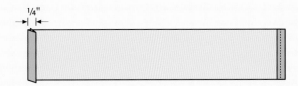

3. Fold the strip in half lengthwise, wrong sides together. Baste the raw edges together to form a tube.

4. Center the raw edge of the strip along the top edge of the quilt back. Pin the sleeve in place.

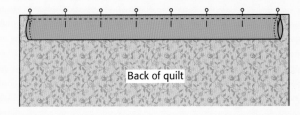

Back of quilt

5. Bind the quilt as instructed in "Binding" (below), securing the sleeve in the seam.

6. After the binding is folded to the back and hand stitched in place, slip-stitch the bottom of the sleeve to the quilt backing. Be careful not to stitch through to the front of the quilt.

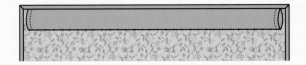

Binding

Binding finishes the edges of quilts. The binding we use is often referred to as double binding because it's folded in half before it's stitched to the edges. It is an easy and secure way to finish your project.

1. Cut the required number of strips as instructed for each individual project. Cut the strips across the width of the fabric.

2. Place two strips right sides together so that they are perpendicular to each other as shown. Draw a diagonal line on the top strip that extends from the point where the upper edges meet to the opposite point where the lower edges meet. Stitch along this line.

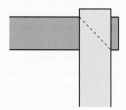

3. Trim the seam allowance to ¼". Press the seam allowance open. Add the remaining strips in the same manner to make one length that is long enough to go around your project.

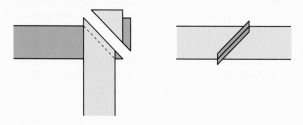

4. When all of the strips have been joined, cut one end at a 45° angle. This will be the beginning of the strip. Press the binding in half lengthwise, wrong sides together, aligning the raw edges.

5. Beginning with the angled end, place the binding strip along one edge of the right side of the quilt top. Align the raw edges and don't start near a corner. Leaving the first 8" of the binding unstitched, stitch the binding to the quilt. Use a ¼" seam allowance. Stop stitching ¼" from the corner. Backstitch and remove the quilt from the machine.

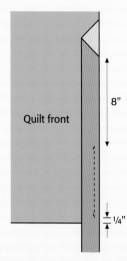

6. Turn the project so that you are ready to sew the next side. Fold the binding up so that it creates a 45°-angle fold.

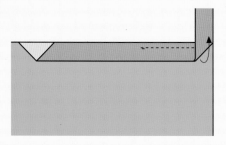

7. Place your finger on the fold to keep it in place; then fold the binding back down so that the new fold is even with the top edge of the quilt and the binding raw edge is aligned with the next side of the quilt. Beginning at the edge, stitch the binding to the quilt, stopping ¼" from the next corner. Repeat the folding and stitching process for each corner.

8. When you are 8" to 12" from your starting point, stop stitching and remove the quilt from the machine. Cut the end of the binding strip so that it overlaps the beginning of the binding strip by at least 5". Pin the ends together 3½" from the starting point. Clip the binding raw edges at the pin, being careful not to cut past the seam allowance or into the quilt layers.

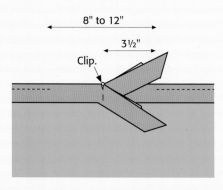

Open up the binding and match the ends as
[sho]wn, right sides together. Stitch the binding strips
[tog]ether on the diagonal.

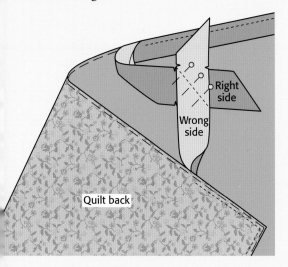

Quilt back

Right
side

Wrong
side

[?]. Refold the binding and check to make sure it
[fits] the quilt. Trim the binding ends to ¼". Finish
[stit]ching the binding to the edge.

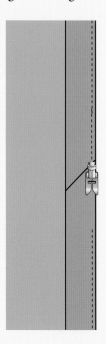

11. Fold the binding over the raw edges to the back
of the quilt. Slip-stitch the binding to the backing
along the fold, mitering the corners.

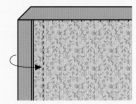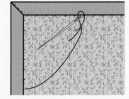

Blocking

This blocking technique ensures your project looks its
best and lies perfectly flat.

1. Using a spray bottle filled with water, heavily mist
your project from both sides and smooth it out with
your hand.

2. Brush the entire project with a lint brush. This
removes any stray threads of fuzz and helps to smooth
out small creases.

3. If the quilt is not square, gently stretch and pin it
to a flat surface to square it up. Let the quilt dry.

Signing Your Quilt

Your quilt isn't finished unless it's signed. You may
think this is unnecessary and a time-consuming step,
but you'll thank yourself for it later. As hard as we
try, we often forget when we completed a project.
Use a permanent-ink pen or fabric marker to put the
following information onto a label:

- Maker's name
- Address
- Date started and completed
- Any special occasion or reason for making the
  quilt

Someday you'll appreciate having this information
on your finished project.

Our designing career started in 1997 when we began wholesaling patterns. We went on to have quilts published in *American Patchwork and Quilting,* and this is our fifth book published with Martingale & Company. In 2004, we began designing fabric for RJR Fabrics. Our first fabric line, "Love Joy Peace," was released in the fall of 2005. At that same time we began designing under our new name, Blue Meadow Designs. You can find more information about us on our Web site, www.bluemeadowdesigns.com. We love hearing from our readers! It's such an encouragement to hear what they like and the projects they have made. We enjoy teaching, speaking, presenting our trunk show, and have begun hosting an annual event called Hometown Retreat. We've enjoyed our quilting journey so far and are looking forward to the many new adventures to come.

Our other books include *Down in the Valley, All through the Woods, Traditional Quilts to Paper Piece,* and *Four Seasons of Quilts.*

CORI DERKSEN

I live on an acreage west of Winkler, Manitoba, Canada, with my husband, Randy; daughter, Kierra; and son, Lane. During the spring and summer months I spend a lot of time gardening and keeping a large yard. During the long winters I like to create scrapbooks and quilts.

MYRA HARDER

I live in Winkler, Manitoba, Canada, with my husband, Mark; son, Samson; and daughter, Robyn. During our short summers, you'll find my family spending as much time as we can at the lake. And during our very long winters, while my husband and children are out playing in the snow, I love to do a little drawing, design a quilt, or read a good book.